COOKING WITH A FOOD PROCESSOR

by

GENERAL ELECTRIC

Grateful thanks to the
Home Economics' staff:

Fay C. Carpenter
Nijole J. Ishkanian
M. Jean O'Donnell
Elizabeth G. Walsh

Pictured: Barbara Tucker, Fay Carpenter

Welcome to the world of Food Processing! Whether you love to cook, hate to cook or fall somewhere in between, your Food Processor will be a valuable kitchen helper. Food processing is fast and as with any new appliance there are basic use techniques that are important to learn and practice. Also, the results may be somewhat different from your present methods.

This cookbook was written specifically with you in mind and contains step-by-step and how-to techniques as well as over 350 photographs and over 200 recipes.

The how-to techniques, and recipes, which include both family favorites and classic dishes, were tested in the General Electric kitchens using a GE Food Processor plus Blender, Model FP2.

If you own a GE Food Processor, Model FP1, the Blender recipes may be prepared in another household blender, although times and results may not be the same. If your Food Processor is not a General Electric, use techniques will be different and you may not get the same results. However, you will find the book useful and informative.

As you become more familiar with your Food Processor, you'll use it more and more. It does the work and lets you get into the fun things fast!

Barbara D. Tucker

Barbara D. Tucker

Contents

The Food Processor: Amazing Work Saver

With just one Knife, one Disc and a Blender, the General Electric Food Processor can mince, chop, grate, grind, shred, slice, blend, purée, liquefy and crush ice.

It performs the time-consuming and tedious jobs which once took the fun out of cooking. Use it daily to save time and work, and give new variety to meals.

A food processor can stretch your food dollars, too. For example, from one 7-pound picnic shoulder you can make croquettes for family dinner, ham spread for a party appetizer, ham and swiss muffins for lunch or supper, and still have enough meat left on the bone for your favorite hearty bean soup.

THE FOOD PROCESSOR DOES ALL THESE JOBS

Shreds cabbage for cole slaw with little effort. Makes the dressing, too.

Slices potatoes for a crowd-size casserole of scalloped potatoes.

Shreds natural Swiss or Cheddar cheese. It's fresher and so easy.

Makes homemade pastry dough for pies in less than a minute.

Chops 1 pound of beef in less than 60 seconds for truly fresh hamburger.

Slices ingredients quickly for an oriental specialty.

Grinds nuts quickly. It helps take the work out of holiday baking.

Turns last night's leftovers into a delicious sandwich spread.

Speeds up preparation for canning and freezing vegetables in season.

The Food Processor Plus Blender Works For You All Through The Day

The versatile Food Processor plus Blender performs an amazing variety of functions. Keep it in a convenient place on your kitchen counter, where it will be handy to help with food preparation several times a day. It handles small jobs as well as large ones, and most parts are dishwasher safe.

A food processor can contribute to good nutrition, too, because it makes it easier to prepare fresh, wholesome vegetables and fruits. You can chop your own meat and be assured of its quality and freshness, selecting the proportion of fat to lean which suits your needs and tastes.

Crumbs bread and crackers for meat loaf and casserole toppings.

Makes smooth or chunky fresh peanut butter without preservatives.

Juliennes potatoes to give French fries a gourmet touch.

Grates Parmesan cheese freshly for authentic Italian main dishes.

Chops and mixes ingredients in one operation for a smooth blend of flavors.

Mixes cakes, including the moist ones which call for shredded vegetables.

Grates chocolate for special desserts.

Purées some of your family dinner to make fresh, homemade baby food.

Gives variety to vegetables. They look different sliced or shredded.

Crushes ice in the Blender for cold beverages, frappes and slushes.

Prepares hollandaise, mayonnaise, and other classic gourmet sauces.

Makes a stunning variety of Blender milk shakes to suit everyone's taste.

Mixes together a quick and easy dip for unexpected guests.

Mixes the dough for a loaf of yeast bread or 1½ dozen dinner rolls.

Purées hearty soups for supper.

Homogenizes salad dressings instead of mixing them by hand.

Slices fruits for pies, salads, fruit plates, main dishes or desserts.

Prepares stuffings for turkey or other poultry, pork chops and fish.

Chops meat for breakfast sausage patties, seasoned to your taste.

Liquefies fruits and vegetables for a refreshing Blender drink.

Mixes up a quick batch of cookies for a party or after-school treat.

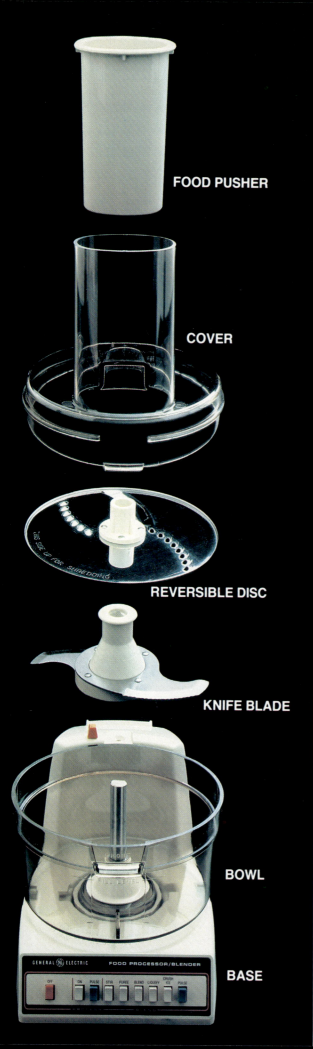

FOOD PUSHER

COVER

REVERSIBLE DISC

KNIFE BLADE

BOWL

BASE

Get To Know Your Food Processor

The General Electric Food Processor plus Blender is a compact, simple to operate kitchen helper. Everything but the base, center post, Blender blades and rubber rings can be washed in the dishwasher. Parts fit together neatly, so you won't need a special storage box to keep the sharp Processor Blade and Disc in a safe place.

The food pusher fits into the food chute. Always use it. When slicing or shredding, it allows you to vary pressure when using the Disc to suit the type of food you are processing and keeps food from splashing out of the food chute when using the Knife Blade.

The cover is made of see-through, crack-resistant Lexan® thermal plastic and has an interlock system which helps assure correct assembly before the Processor will operate. The extra tall food chute allows you to load a little or a lot of food for slicing or shredding, or to add ingredients while processing.

The Knife Blade and Reversible Disc fit onto the center post. They can be used separately or together.

The Bowl is also made of Lexan plastic. The center post with rubber ring fits into the Bowl and is held in place with a screw-on ring. Liquids can't leak out between Bowl and post, yet the Bowl comes apart easily for cleaning.

A compact dual purpose base houses the motor which runs both the Processor and the Blender. In the center of the base is a round well, into which you can fit either the Processor Bowl or the Blender Jar.

The buttons are arranged so they are easy to understand and use. The **Off** button stops both Processor and Blender. Two buttons operate the Processor: **On,** for continuous processing, and **Pulse** for short bursts of action. The Blender has **five** speeds and a **Pulse** button, which is used in the same way as the Processor Pulse, and operates at the high, Crush Ice speed. Here are some suggested uses for the Blender speeds:

SPEED	USES
Stir	Mixing thin batters, instant puddings, scrambled eggs, gravies and marinades.
Puree	Puréeing cooked or uncooked fruits, vegetables and small amounts of cooked meats. Making baby foods for special diets.
Blend	Dips, salad dressings, crumbing breads/crackers, dessert toppings or mousses.
Liquefy	Drinks, frappes, thick mixtures, spreads, smoothing soups, sauces.
Crush Ice	Crushing ice cubes in drinks, for ice cones. Also for grinding coffee beans, delumping sugar, grating chocolate, hard cheese and mixing extra thick mixtures.

THE BLENDER AND PROCESSOR ATTACHMENTS OFFER A VARIETY OF RESULTS

When you use the Blender and Processor to simplify and speed up food preparation, choose the method which will give the results you want. The directions and recipes in this book are accompanied by symbols to help you select the right attachment for every task.

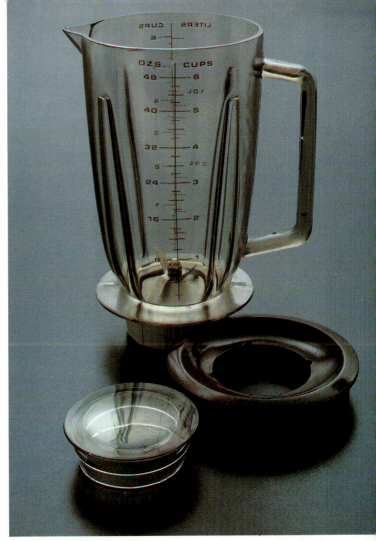

The Knife Blade minces, chops, grinds, mixes and purées, depending on the type of food and processing method you use. Always grasp the Knife Blade by its center hub and remove it before emptying Bowl.

The Blender blends up to 4½ cups of liquid. It mixes liquid and dry ingredients. Use it to crush ice, purée fruits and vegetables, liquefy foods, make drinks and stir light mixtures.

The slicing side of the Disc slices vegetables, fruits, cooked or partially frozen meats, firm cheese, or coarsely shreds cabbage. By slicing foods twice you can produce a julienne or matchstick-cut (page 15).

The shredding side makes either short or long shreds, depending upon the way you load the food chute. Use it at the same time as the Knife Blade for fine grating.

FACTORS THAT AFFECT FOOD PROCESSING

Size. When chopping, quarter foods or cut them in 1-inch pieces. Large pieces chop unevenly, with some particles coarse and others overprocessed. For slicing and shredding, foods which are too large for the food chute must be cut to fit it. Try to buy foods which fit the chute whole or that require just a little hand cutting.

Quality. Fresh, crisp or firm fruits and vegetables process best. That doesn't mean you can't use up an old carrot or limp piece of celery, but you should not expect the same results that you get with fresh produce.

Quantity. Medium-sized loads chop more evenly than large ones. If your recipe calls for 4 medium onions, chop them 2 at a time; it only takes a few seconds longer and food will be evenly chopped without being overprocessed. A large load gives uneven results.

Temperature. Fruits, vegetables and medium-hard cheeses should be processed at refrigerator temperature. Process Parmesan and Romano cheese at room temperature. For slicing, raw meat should be partially frozen until it is firm, but not solid.

Pressure. The amount of pressure you apply on the pusher varies depending on the firmness of the food you are slicing or shredding and the results desired. For most foods, steady, even pressure is needed.

Use firm pressure on the food pusher for hard foods, such as lemons. Always be sure to position the pusher before starting to process.

Light pressure should be used for soft foods, such as strawberries. Cucumbers and potatoes will self-feed without pressure for thinner, but slightly irregular pieces.

Pulsing. For most chopping, use the Pulse button. Press it and release immediately. Short spurts of action stir food as it is chopped, giving more even results. One or two Pulses may be enough for coarse chopping.

Medium chopping requires just a few more Pulses, depending on the amount and type of food. Check food often to avoid over-chopping.

Fine chopping can be started with a few Pulses, then finished with longer ones. Stop and scrape down Bowl with a spatula. Wetter foods sometimes stick to sides of Bowl.

LOADING THE FOOD CHUTE FOR SLICING ● AND SHREDDING ⊛

Pack food chute for best results when slicing long, narrow foods. Cut food to fit chute, (about 5-inch lengths). Wedge pieces in chute, alternating thick and thin ends. This method results in short shreds and round slices.

Slice a single food by positioning it on the left side of chute (OFF button side). Hold it in place with pusher. The Disc's clockwise rotation pushes the food against the left wall of the chute, which helps to hold it upright.

Arrange 2½-inch pieces horizontally in the chute for long shreds, which are attractive in salads, or for long slices used in Oriental dishes or for vegetable dips.

Try loading chute from the bottom when slicing. Bottom of chute is larger than the top, so food which won't fit the top may fit the bottom. For neater slices, cut a small slice off one end of food so it rests flat on Disc.

Place small foods, or short pieces, which will stand upright, directly on the Disc to simplify arrangement. Carefully position food chute over them and slice.

Place meat on cookie sheet in freezer until partially frozen (page 30). Then cut meat to fit food chute. Use pusher as a guide. Slice, using firm pressure on pusher. Result is thinly sliced meat for casseroles and stir-fries.

HOW-TO LESSONS DEMONSTRATE BASIC PROCESSING TECHNIQUES

Before you can use your Food Processor to perform all its tasks, you should learn a few simple techniques. These lessons demonstrate each one, using typical foods. Apply them to other similar foods for similar results.

In general, mince and chop using a dry Knife Blade and dry Bowl. If you want several cups of food coarsely and evenly chopped, do them in 1-cup batches, even when the maximum capacity is 2 cups. When slicing, shredding or julienning, empty Bowl as food reaches Fill Level.

HOW TO CHOP ⌀

Quarter peeled onions. (Cut large ones in eighths.) Position Knife Blade in dry Bowl; add up to two medium onions. Pulse to chop.

Coarse chopping of 1 medium onion takes about 2 to 4 Pulses. Coarsely chopped onions process more evenly 1 onion at a time.

Fine chopping takes about 2 or 3 more Pulses. Scrape Bowl once during chopping. Drain onions, if needed.

HOW TO CRUMB ⌀ or ⊕

Method 1: Break up to 4 slices **fresh** bread in quarters. Position Knife Blade in Bowl. Add bread. Process until crumbed to fineness desired.

Method 2: Position Disc in Bowl with shredding side up. Fold 1 or 2 slices of fresh bread in half. Place in food chute and shred.

Use Knife Blade for coarse crumbs. For fine crumbs, use either method, depending on which attachment you plan to use again in the recipe.

HOW TO GRATE ⌀ ⊕

Position Knife Blade in dry Bowl with Disc above it, shredding side up. Cut room temperature Parmesan or Romano cheese to fit chute.

Place cheese in chute. If you can't insert a knife point in cheese easily, it's too hard to process. Cheese is shredded and grated at the same time.

Process until texture of cheese is as fine as you wish. To save clean-up, grate cheese before chopping or slicing other messier foods.

HOW TO JULIENNE

Slice potatoes. Remove potato slices from Bowl. Hold cover sideways, with pusher inserted part way to form a cup at the bottom of the chute.

Wedge slices in chute with cut edges at right angles to cover. Pack them tightly so they will not fall out when cover is placed on Bowl.

Reposition Disc with slicing side up. Slice potatoes again. Repeat with remaining slices. Cross-cutting produces the julienne or matchstick-cut.

HOW TO MINCE

Position Knife Blade in dry Bowl. Foods will not mince as finely in wet Bowl. Place cover on Processor.

Drop peeled garlic clove through food chute with Processor running. Quickly cover chute. It takes 3 to 5 seconds.

Use this method to mince small items, such as 1-inch pieces of carrot or onion, or a ½-inch piece of ginger root.

HOW TO PURÉE IN THE BLENDER

Drain cooked fruits or vegetables; save liquid. Add up to 3 cups food and ¼ cup or more liquid for each cup.

Blend at Puree speed until food is as smooth as desired. You may need to stop and stir mixture once or twice.

Blended purées may have a slightly smoother texture than Processor purées, especially small quantities.

HOW TO PURÉE IN THE PROCESSOR ∾

Drain cooked fruit and vegetables, reserving liquid. Position Knife Blade in Bowl. Add from ½ to 3 cups food and ¼ cup liquid for each cup.

Add butter or seasonings to purée if desired. Thin with a little liquid, if purée is too thick.

Process until food reaches desired fineness. If necessary, stop processing to scrape down Bowl with spatula. Repeat until all food is processed.

HOW TO SHRED ⊕

Position Disc in Bowl with shredding side up. Cut food to fit food chute.

Place food and pusher in chute. For hard and medium-hard natural cheese, use light pressure.

Shred cheese or other food. When shredding large quantities, empty Bowl as food reaches Fill Level.

HOW TO SLICE ⊙

Position Disc in Bowl with slicing side up. Halve cucumbers crosswise. Remove ends and peel if desired.

Place half a cucumber upright in food chute. Slice. Remember to empty Bowl as slices reach Fill Level.

Use firm pressure for even slices. Cucumbers may be halved lengthwise and seeded if desired.

SAVE CLEAN UP...
ORGANIZE YOUR PROCESSING

Bowl washing is rarely necessary when processing several ingredients separately for the same recipe, but food processing is even faster if you organize your processing to cut down on clean up. If you're making a main dish, a salad and a dessert, prepare ingredients for all of them in good processing order and clean up only once.

First, process ingredients that need a dry Bowl and Knife, such as parsley, Parmesan cheese or bread crumbs.

Next, mince small items like garlic or a chunk of carrot. Then chop larger quantities, such as an onion or green pepper. Chopping works better in a dry Bowl, too.

After chopping, slice or shred vegetables; they don't need a dry Bowl. Slice or shred cheese after vegetables since cheese pieces sometimes stick to the Disc.

Last, process fatty foods like chopped beef. Clean up.

For example, here's how you would prepare a meatloaf, cole slaw and chopped nuts for a brownie mix with only one Bowl washing.

Position Disc in Bowl with slicing side up. Add walnuts to food chute. Slice and add to brownie mix.

Position Disc in Bowl with shredding side up. Fold 1 slice fresh bread in half. Shred. Set aside in mixing bowl.

Position Knife Blade in Bowl. Chop enough onion for both meatloaf and cole slaw. Add some to mixing bowl and some to salad bowl.

Position Disc in Bowl with shredding side up. Shred carrot for cole slaw. Add to salad bowl.

Position Disc in Bowl with slicing side up. Slice cabbage. Empty into salad bowl as it reaches Fill Level.

Position Knife Blade in Bowl. Add 1 cup cubed beef. Pulse, 5 to 10 seconds. Add to mixing bowl and chop remaining beef. Then wash Bowl.

17

Food Processing from A to Z

With the Food Processor, one attachment performs a variety of tasks. For example, the Knife Blade can mince, chop, grind, mix or purée. The differences in the results obtained depend on the character of the food and the method used in processing.

On the following pages you'll find instructions for ways to process a broad selection of foods. Color photographs will show you the results you can expect when you follow the simple directions.

ALMONDS: Ground

Position Knife Blade in very dry Bowl. Add up to 1 cup nuts. Hard nuts process even better when frozen.

Pulse until nuts are the texture desired. Above, coarsely ground. Hard nuts include almonds, cashews, filberts and peanuts.

Ground nuts can be processed as fine as you wish. If a very fine grind is needed for baking, add ¼ cup flour from recipe before processing.

APPLES: Chopped

Quarter apples. Peel, if desired. Cut each quarter in half crosswise. If apples are large, cut quarters in thirds. Position Knife Blade in Bowl.

Add up to 1 cup apple pieces to Bowl. Pulse until apple is chopped to desired texture. Check often.

Coarsely chopped apple takes about 5 seconds, finely chopped, about 7. Repeat to chop remaining amount.

APPLES: Sliced

Quarter and core apples. Peel, if desired. Position Disc in Bowl with slicing side up.

Stack apple quarters in food chute horizontally. For neat slices, slice 2 quarters at a time with flat side on Disc. Repeat with remaining quarters.

Use firm pressure for even slices. Sprinkle with lemon juice to prevent browning or use immediately.

ARTICHOKES, Jerusalem, Peeled: Sliced. See POTATOES, page 41

ASPARAGUS, Fresh: Sliced. See CELERY, page 24

AVOCADOS, Peeled, Pitted: Sliced. See PEARS, page 38

BANANAS: Mashed

Cut ripe bananas into 1-inch pieces. Place from ½ to 3 bananas in Blender Jar. Blend at Puree speed.

Scrape down side of Bowl when mashing ½ to 3 ripe bananas (cut in 1-inch pieces) in Processor.

Blended bananas are somewhat smoother than Processor bananas, especially small quantities.

BANANAS: Sliced

Peel banana and cut in half. Position Disc in Bowl with slicing side up.

Place banana halves in chute with cut side against Disc. Use light pressure.

Coat sliced bananas with citrus juice to prevent browning, or serve at once.

BEANS, Snap: French-Cut

Cut off ends and cut beans in 2- to 2½-inch lengths. Position Disc in Bowl with slicing side up.

Stack beans in food chute, horizontally, using a spatula to help arrange them. Slice, using light pressure.

Beans may also be blanched five minutes before slicing, then briefly cooked before serving.

BEEF: See MEAT, page 30, 31

BEETS: Sliced

Cook whole, washed beets with 1 or 2 inches of top and root left on. Cool, trim and remove skins.

Position Disc in Bowl, slicing side up. Cut beets to fit food chute, if necessary, and slice.

Slice only cooked or canned beets. If top and skin are removed before cooking, color will "bleed."

BRAZIL NUTS: Chopped. See WALNUTS, page 45

BREAD, Dry: Crumbs

Position Knife Blade in dry Bowl, with Disc above it, shredding side up. Break bread into pieces.

Place bread in chute. Process until crumbed. If any pieces remain on Disc, add to Bowl; process. (Or crumb 1 cup of 2-inch pieces in Blender.)

Store dry bread crumbs in the refrigerator. Crumbing is a good use for stale bread, or leftover garlic bread.

BREAD CRUMBS, Fresh: See HOW TO CRUMB, page 14

BUTTER: See Homemade Butter recipe, page 105

CABBAGE: Chopped

Cut cored cabbage in 1-inch pieces. Position Knife Blade in Bowl.

Add up to 2 handfuls of pieces to Bowl. Pulse until cabbage reaches desired fineness. Repeat as needed.

Check coarsely chopped cabbage after 2 seconds. Scrape down Bowl once or twice when chopping finely.

CABBAGE: Shredded

Cut cabbage in pieces to fit food chute; remove cores. Position Disc in Bowl, with slicing side up.

Drop pieces in chute. Slice. Empty Bowl as cabbage reaches Fill Level.

Result is coarsely shredded cabbage for cole slaw or soups. Shredding Disc will produce very fine shreds.

CABBAGE, Chinese: Shredded. See CABBAGE: Shredded, above

CARROTS: Chopped

Cut peeled carrots in 1-inch lengths; cut large pieces in half. Position Knife Blade in Bowl.

Add up to 2 cups carrots to Bowl. Pulse until carrots are chopped to desired texture.

Coarsely chopped carrots process more evenly in 1-cup batches.

CARROTS: Julienned

Slice peeled carrots horizontally as directed on page 12 for long slices. Stack carrot slices; reposition Disc with slicing side up.

Hold cover sideways with pusher inserted to form a shallow cup. Wedge slices in horizontally with cut sides of stack at right angles to cover.

Slice again. Cross-cutting produces julienne or matchstick-cut carrots. This works best with larger, fat carrots.

CARROTS: Shredded. See HOW TO SHRED, page 16 and LOADING THE FOOD CHUTE..., page 12

CARROTS: Sliced. See HOW TO SLICE, page 16 and LOADING THE FOOD CHUTE..., page 12

CASHEWS: Ground. See ALMONDS, page 18

CAULIFLOWER: Sliced ⊘

Divide cauliflower into flowerets. Position Disc in Bowl, slicing side up.

Arrange flowerets in chute, alternating heads and stems. (Wedge large pieces up from bottom of chute.) Slice, using moderate pressure.

Do not discard bits of crumbled cauliflower. Add them with slices to salads, casseroles or sauces.

CELERY: Chopped. See CARROTS, page 23

CELERY: Sliced ⊘

Remove strings from celery. Cut each stalk crosswise in thirds. If base is very broad, slit lengthwise 1 or 2 inches.

Position Disc in Bowl, slicing side up. Place celery pieces upright in chute. Slice, using firm pressure.

Celery slices are even. For best results, slice more than one stalk at a time and tightly pack food chute.

CELERY ROOT, (Knob), Peeled: Shredded, sliced. See POTATOES, page 40, 41

CHEESE, Hard: Grated. See HOW TO GRATE, page 14

CHEESE, Medium Hard: Shredded, sliced. See HOW TO SHRED, SLICE, page 16

CHEESE, Soft: Crumbled 🌀

Break chilled Blue, Feta or Mozzarella cheese in 1-inch pieces. Position Knife Blade in Bowl.

Drop up to 5 pieces through chute with motor running. Process just until crumbled, about 5 seconds.

Use crumbled cheese in salads, casseroles or dips. Do not try to crumble soft, moist cheeses.

CHICKEN: See MEAT, page 30, 31

CHOCOLATE: Grated 🥤

Quarter 1 square of room temperature chocolate. Place the quarters in Blender Jar. Cover; blend at Crush Ice speed 5 to 10 seconds.

Place ½ cup room temperature chocolate bits in Blender Jar. Cover; blend at Crush Ice speed 10 seconds.

Add grated chocolate to cake batters and frostings, or use to decorate cakes. Chocolate can be grated in Processor; it takes a little longer.

COCONUT, Fresh: Shredded ⚫

Remove brown husk from coconut and cut meat in pieces to fit chute.

Position Disc in Bowl with shredding side up. Place coconut in chute; shred, using firm pressure.

Use freshly shredded coconut in baking or as a condiment for curries.

COCONUT, Fresh: Grated. See HOW TO GRATE, page 14

COOKIES: Crumbs. See BREAD, Dry, page 21

CRACKERS: Crumbs. See BREAD, Dry, page 21

CRANBERRIES: Chopped. See OLIVES, page 34

CREAM, Whipping or Heavy: Thickened 〰️

Position Knife Blade in Bowl. Pour in up to 1 cup whipping cream. (For best results, use day-old cream.)

Process until thickened, checking after 20 to 25 seconds. Sweeten with 1 to 2 tablespoons confectioners' sugar, if desired.

Serve over strawberries, gingerbread or other desserts. Thickened cream will not be fluffy like whipped cream.

CUCUMBERS: Chopped

Halve cucumber lengthwise; peel if desired. Scoop out seeds if they are tough. Cut into 1-inch pieces.

Position Knife Blade in Bowl. Add up to 2 cups cucumber pieces. Pulse several times until chopped.

Check chopped cucumber frequently to avoid overprocessing. Drain before using in recipe, if necessary.

CUCUMBERS: Julienned

Slice cucumbers with firm pressure. Remove and stack slices. Reposition Disc with slicing side up. Hold cover sideways with pusher inserted part way to form a cup.

Wedge slices in tightly with cut edges at right angles to cover. Carefully place cover on Bowl and slice again.

Repeat with remaining slices. Use julienne or matchstick-cut cucumbers in salads, sauces or relishes.

CUCUMBERS: Shredded ⚫

Cut cucumbers to fit food chute. If seeds are tough, halve lengthwise; scoop out seeds. Peel if desired.

Position Disc in Bowl with shredding side up. Put cucumber and pusher in food chute; then shred.

Use shredded cucumber in relishes, salads and fish sauces.

CUCUMBERS: Sliced. See HOW TO SLICE, page 16

EGGPLANT: Julienned. See CUCUMBERS, page 27

EGGPLANT: Sliced ⚫

Quarter eggplant or cut in pieces to fit food chute. Peel, if desired. Position Disc in Bowl, slicing side up.

Place eggplant in food chute. Slice, using firm pressure. Empty Bowl as slices reach Fill Level.

Place eggplant in colander over sink or bowl. Salt lightly; let stand 10 minutes to remove excess moisture.

EGGS, Hard Cooked: Chopped 👁️

Peel, dry and halve hard-cooked eggs. Position Knife Blade in Bowl.

Add from ½ to 6 eggs. Pulse until eggs are chopped to desired texture.

Check after 2 to 3 Pulses. Eggs chop quickly. Use the same method to chop egg yolks alone.

FILBERTS: Ground. See ALMONDS, page 18

FISH, Boned Raw/Scallops: See HOW TO MAKE CHOPPED RAW BEEF, page 71 (Chop 2 cups at once.)

FRUIT, Candied or Dry: Chopped 👁️

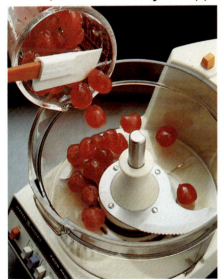

Position Knife Blade in Bowl. Add up to 2 cups pitted fruit or raisins.

Add ½ cup flour per cup of fruit. Pulse 3 seconds. Check frequently and do not overprocess.

Remember to subtract the flour used in processing fruit from the amount of flour in your recipe.

GARLIC: Minced. See HOW TO MINCE, page 15

GINGER ROOT: Minced. See HOW TO MINCE, page 15

HAM: See MEAT, page 30, 31

HORSERADISH: Grated. See HOW TO GRATE, page 14

JICAMA: Sliced, shredded. See POTATOES, page 40, 41

LAMB: See MEAT, page 30, 31

LEEKS: Chopped, sliced. See ONIONS, Green, page 35, 36

LEMONS: Sliced

Choose a lemon small enough to fit bottom of food chute for whole slices. Cut off one end. Position Disc in Bowl with slicing side up.

Load food chute from bottom with cut side of lemon down. Place small lemon upright on left side of Disc, (page 12). Slice, using firm pressure.

Result is whole, neat lemon slices. If lemon is too large for chute, cut a slice off one side or cut in half.

LETTUCE: See CABBAGE, page 22 (Do not use shredding side of Disc with lettuce.)

LIMES: Sliced. See LEMONS, above

MEAT, Boneless and Uncooked: Sliced

Spread boned meat on cookie sheet and place in freezer until partially frozen (firm, but not solid). Cut thick pieces of meat to fit food chute. Roll up thin, flat ones.

Position Disc in Bowl with slicing side up. Insert meat through bottom of chute. Pack chute for best results. Slice, using firm pressure.

Sliced meat is ready to cook in stir-fries and casseroles. Check meat often while partially freezing. Do not slice meat which is solidly frozen.

MEAT, Cooked: Chopped

Cut chilled cooked meat in 1-inch pieces. Remove gristle and fat. Position Knife Blade in Bowl.

Add up to 2 cups meat pieces. Pulse until meat is chopped as desired.

Chop meat coarsely for salads and main dishes, finely for spreads.

MEAT, Cooked: Sliced. See SAUSAGE, Hard, page 42

MEAT, Uncooked: Chopped. See HOW TO MAKE CHOPPED RAW BEEF, page 71

MEAT, Packaged, Sliced: Cross Cut

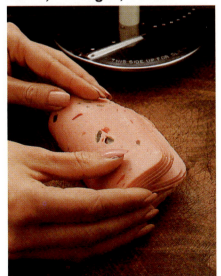 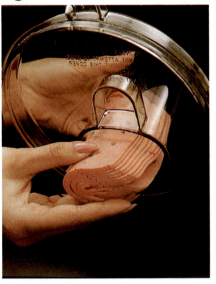 

Stack several slices of boiled ham, bologna, soft (not hard) salami or other lunch meat. (8-ounce package works best.) Roll or fold stack.

Wedge roll up bottom of food chute. Position Disc in Bowl with slicing side up. Slice.

Use cross cut meats in chef salads, sandwich spreads or soups.

MELONS: Sliced 🌀

Halve and seed melon. Cut pieces to fit food chute and remove rind. Position Disc in Bowl, slicing side up.

Pack melon in food chute. Slice, using moderate pressure. Empty Bowl as slices reach Fill Level.

Use sliced melon in salads, fruit cups and oriental dishes.

MUSHROOMS: Chopped 👁🌀

Position Knife Blade in Bowl with Disc above it, slicing side up. Wash, but do not stem mushrooms.

Slice as many as 5 or 6 mushrooms, using Pulse button; then Pulse until mushrooms are chopped to desired texture. Remove mushrooms and repeat with second batch, if needed.

Check after 1 or 2 Pulses when chopping mushrooms coarsely. Fine chopping will take about 8 to 10 seconds. To chop with Knife Blade alone, halve or quarter mushrooms.

MUSHROOMS: Sliced 🟤

Cut a slice off one side of 2 mushroom caps. Position Disc in Bowl, slicing side up. Place cut sides of mushrooms directly on Disc in the area beneath chute; then cover.

Stack remaining mushrooms sideways in chute, alternating caps and stems. Use spatula to arrange them tightly. Slice with firm pressure.

Use mushroom slices for salads and garnishes. For soups and stews, when appearance is not important, mushrooms may be loaded in the chute without careful placement.

NECTARINES: Sliced. See PEACHES, page 37

NUTS, Hard: Ground. See ALMONDS, page 18

NUTS, Soft: Chopped. See WALNUTS, page 45

OKRA: Sliced 🟤

Remove ends and cut in half crosswise if necessary. Position Disc in Bowl with slicing side up.

Pack okra upright in food chute, alternating thick and thin ends. Slice.

Use sliced okra in gumbos and other Creole dishes, or for frying.

OLIVES: Chopped

Position Knife Blade in Bowl. Add up to 1 cup pitted or stuffed olives. Processing time will depend on the number and size of olives chopped.

Chop olives coarsely by Pulsing once or twice. Check texture; scrape down Bowl. Pulse again, if necessary. Check after every Pulse.

Finely chopped olives take just a few seconds longer than coarsely chopped. Check often and scrape Bowl with a spatula as needed.

OLIVES: Sliced

Position Disc in Bowl with slicing side up. Arrange pitted or stuffed olives, open end down, on Disc in the area beneath the food chute.

Place chute over olives and slice, using moderate pressure.

Olives vary in quality. Select large firm ones for neat, attractive slices.

ONIONS: Chopped. See HOW TO CHOP, page 14

ONIONS: Sliced 🌓

Peel onions; slice off ends. For rings, choose onions small enough to fit up food chute from bottom. Halve large ones from root to stem.

Position Disc in Bowl with slicing side up. Insert onion through bottom of food chute with root end down. If halved, wedge in chute upright. Slice, using firm pressure.

Whole, small onions produce rings. Cut ones make half-slices. Very large ones may need to be quartered.

ONIONS, Green (Scallions): Chopped 👁

Remove roots and all but 3 inches of green tops from onions. Cut onions in 1-inch pieces.

Position Knife Blade in Bowl. Add up to 2 cups onions. Pulse, checking frequently, until onions are evenly chopped. Scrape Bowl as needed.

Expect processed onions to have a different texture from hand chopped. Some pieces will be slightly longer.

ONIONS, Green (Scallions): Sliced

Remove roots and soft part of tops. Cut onions in 3 equal pieces. Position Disc in Bowl, slicing side up.

Place onions upright in food chute. Pack as tightly as possible and slice.

Use sliced green onions in salads, quiches and casseroles.

ORANGES: Sliced

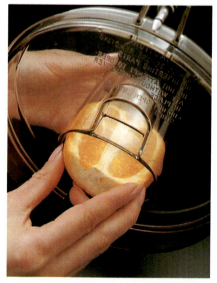

Cut a slice off one end of orange. If orange is too large to fit up bottom of food chute, halve lengthwise by cutting straight down through stem.

Position Disc in Bowl with slicing side up. Insert orange through bottom of chute lengthwise, with sliced end down. Slice, using firm pressure.

Use orange slices on fruit plates or to garnish fruit punches and drinks.

PARSLEY: Chopped and Minced

Wash parsley and dry very thoroughly. Wet parsley will not process well. Cut leaves from stems.

Position dry Knife Blade in dry Bowl. Add parsley leaves. Process until parsley is chopped or minced evenly.

Store chopped parsley in plastic bag or container in refrigerator. It should stay fresh at least a week. Parsley can also be frozen.

PARSNIPS: See HOW TO SLICE, SHRED, page 16

PEACHES: Sliced

Peel, halve and pit firm, ripe peaches. Position Disc in Bowl with slicing side up.

Position 1 to 2 peach halves in chute. Slice, using firm pressure on pusher.

Sprinkle peaches with lemon juice to prevent browning, or use at once.

PEANUTS: Ground. See ALMONDS, page 18

PEARS: Sliced

Quarter and core firm, ripe pears. Position Disc in Bowl, slicing side up.

Arrange pear quarters in food chute, alternating thick and thin ends. Slice, using firm pressure on pusher.

Sprinkle slices with lemon juice to prevent browning or use at once.

PECANS: Chopped. See WALNUTS, page 45

PEPPERONI: Sliced. See SAUSAGE, Hard, page 42

PEPPERS, Sweet, Green or Red: Chopped

Quarter green or red peppers. Remove tops, seeds and pith. Cut quarters crosswise in thirds. Position Knife Blade in Bowl.

Add up to 12 pieces of pepper to Bowl. Pulse until pepper is chopped. Peppers process very quickly.

Drain chopped pepper if necessary before using, except when adding them to soups and sauces where extra moisture is desired.

PEPPERS, Sweet, Green or Red: Sliced 🙂

Remove top from pepper. Halve and seed. If pepper is small enough to fit food chute, remove seeds and pith through top, leaving pepper whole.

Position Disc in Bowl, slicing side up. Insert pepper through bottom of chute, stem side up. Gently squeeze sides of pepper to make it fit. Slice.

Use sliced peppers in salads, stir-fries or as a garnish for meats.

PICKLES: Chopped. See CUCUMBERS, page 27

PICKLES: Sliced 🙂

Cut ends from pickles. Position Disc in Bowl with slicing side up.

Place pickles upright in food chute. Slice, using moderate pressure.

Use sliced pickles to garnish hamburgers, tuna dishes or a relish tray.

PINEAPPLES, Fresh: Sliced 🌀

Remove top from pineapple and cut lengthwise into wedges to fit chute. Remove rind, eyes and core.

Position Disc in Bowl with slicing side up. Pack pineapple wedge in food chute. Slice.

Use pineapple slices in main dishes, fruit cups and salads, but not gelatin, since it prevents setting.

PLANTINS: Sliced. See BANANAS, page 20

PORK: See MEAT, page 30, 31

POTATOES: Chopped. See APPLES, page 18

POTATOES: Julienned. See HOW TO JULIENNE, page 15

POTATOES: Shredded 🌀

Peel potatoes. If they are large, halve, quarter, or cut them to fit food chute.

Position Disc in Bowl with shredding side up. Place potatoes in chute, cut side down. Shred.

Place potato shreds in cold water to prevent darkening. Drain just before cooking. Dry well before frying.

POTATOES: Sliced

Select small potatoes for whole slices. Halve, quarter or cut large ones to fit chute. Peel, if desired.

Position Disc in Bowl, slicing side up. Place potato in chute. Slice. Empty Bowl as slices reach Fill Level.

Sliced potatoes are attractive and more nutritious when left unpeeled.

POTATOES, Sweet: Mashed. See SQUASH, Butternut, page 42

PUMPKIN: Mashed. See SQUASH, Butternut, page 42

RADISHES: Sliced

Remove radish roots and tops. Position Disc in Bowl, slicing side up.

Place radishes in food chute. Slice.

Use radishes in tossed salads, or to garnish egg or potato salads.

RHUBARB: Sliced. See CELERY, page 24

RUTABAGAS: Sliced. See POTATOES, above

SALAMI: Sliced. See SAUSAGE, Hard, page 42

SAUSAGE, Hard: Sliced 🔵

Cut narrow sausage, such as pepperoni or hard salami into 3-inch lengths. Remove inedible casing.

Position Disc in Bowl, slicing side up. Wedge sausage in food chute.

Slice, using firm pressure. Use salami, left, for appetizers and sandwiches, and pepperoni, right, for pizzas.

SCALLIONS: See ONIONS, Green, page 35, 36

SHALLOTS: Minced. See HOW TO MINCE, page 15

SQUASH, Butternut: Mashed 🔵

Halve squash. Remove seeds, fibers and rind. Cut into 1-inch pieces.

Bring 1 inch of salted water to a boil in a pan large enough to hold squash. Add squash; cover and simmer until tender, about 20 minutes.

Drain squash well. Position Knife Blade in Bowl. Process up to 3 cups until very smooth.

SQUASH, Summer: See ZUCCHINI, page 46

STRAWBERRIES: Chopped

Hull berries; halve large ones. Position Knife Blade in Bowl. Add up to 2 cups strawberries.

Pulse 2 or 3 times to chop coarsely. Use chopped strawberries in pies, fruit cups or dessert fillings.

Process about 10 seconds to purée berries. Scrape down Bowl, if necessary. Use strawberry purée in fruit toppings and gelatin desserts.

STRAWBERRIES: Sliced

Hull firm, ripe strawberries. Position Disc in Bowl, slicing side up.

Fill chute, arranging strawberries on their sides for lengthwise slices.

Slice, using very light pressure.

TOMATOES: Chopped

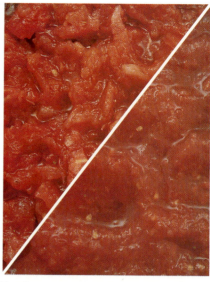

Quarter tomatoes. Remove peel and seeds, if desired.

Position Knife Blade in Bowl. Add up to 8 tomato quarters. Pulse, checking texture frequently.

Drain coarsely chopped tomatoes before using in salads or sandwiches. Add finely chopped, undrained tomatoes to soups, sauces or casseroles.

TOMATOES: Sliced

Select tomatoes small enough to fit bottom of food chute. Peel, if desired, and remove stem end. Position Disc in Bowl with slicing side up.

Insert tomato through bottom of chute. For meatier slices, turn tomato on its side to slice lengthwise.

Slice, using medium pressure. Drain slices before using in salads. Halve larger tomatoes before slicing.

TOMATOES, Plum: Sliced 🌑

Cut off stem end of plum tomato. Peel, if desired. Position Disc in Bowl with slicing side up.

Wedge tomato in food chute or place upright on Disc, depending on size. Slice, using medium pressure.

Plum tomatoes are excellent for slicing because they are small and meaty.

TURNIPS: Sliced. See POTATOES, page 41

WALNUTS: Chopped 🌑 or ◠

Position slicing side of Disc or Knife Blade in Bowl, depending on whether you want to chop coarsely or finely.

Choose slicing side of Disc for coarsely chopped nuts. Place walnuts, pecans or Brazil nuts in food chute.

Use Knife Blade for finely chopped or ground nuts, following directions for almonds, page 18.

WATER CHESTNUTS: Sliced. See RADISHES, page 41

WATERCRESS: Chopped. See PARSLEY, page 37

YAMS: Mashed. See SQUASH, Butternut, page 42

ZUCCHINI: Shredded 🅢

Slice ends from zucchini, then cut to fit food chute horizontally. Process, using shredding side of Disc.

Place zucchini shreds in colander over bowl or sink. Sprinkle lightly with salt; toss. Drain at least 10 minutes.

Squeeze out excess moisture and dry on paper towels. Zucchini shreds will then cook quickly in butter or oil without becoming watery.

ZUCCHINI: Sliced. See HOW TO SLICE, page 16

SOME FOODS DO NOT PROCESS WELL

The Food Processor performs many tasks, but there are a few things it can't do, others that the Blender does better, and some that should not be done either way.

THINGS THE PROCESSOR DOES NOT DO

Beat egg whites with volume.
Whip cream to a thick and fluffy consistency.
Mash potatoes. (They become gluey.)
Slice or shred soft cheeses.
Slice or shred candied or dried fruits.
Slice hard-cooked eggs or hard nuts.

Shred onions or lettuce.
Grind coffee beans.
Liquefy fruits and vegetables.
Crush ice.

THINGS WHICH CAN DAMAGE THE PROCESSOR AND BLENDER:

Cheese which is so hard you have trouble cutting it.
Solidly frozen meat.
Bones and other inedible parts of food.
Spices ground alone, such as whole cloves, which have a high oil content.

COMMON PROBLEMS AND SOLUTIONS

Beginning users of food processors sometimes experience problems. Some of these are unavoidable with food processing, and are more than off-set by the ease with which the processor accomplishes time-consuming or tedious tasks. Some problems are due to inexperience, and will disappear as you become familiar with the appliance.

Before processing a new food, read the instructions in the How-To Lessons, or Food Processing from A to Z.

Problem: Food is unevenly chopped. Processor may move on countertop.
Solution: Bowl is overloaded. Chop this quantity in two or more batches.

Problem: Liquid leaks out between Processor Bowl and cover.
Solution: Limit liquids or semi-liquids to 2 cups or less. Don't overfill.

Problem: Sliced or shredded food comes out chopped.
Solution: Remember to remove the Knife Blade unless you want food to be finely chopped.

Problem: Slices vary in thickness.
Solution: Use pusher for even slices. Cucumbers or potatoes will self-feed without pusher for thin slices, but thickness will be uneven.

Problem: Single foods such as a carrot or lemon fall over in chute.
Solution: Position food at left side of chute to minimize problem. Hold in place with pusher. See page 12.

Problem: Some larger pieces of food drop over side of Disc into the Bowl during shredding.
Solution: This is normal, Remove larger pieces if you object to them.

Problem: Medium-hard cheese may spread out or wad on Disc.
Solution: This is normal. Slice or shred only chilled cheese. Use light pressure on food pusher.

Problem: Shredded or sliced food piles up on one side of Bowl.
Solution: This is normal. When food reaches Fill Level in any area of Bowl, empty it; then continue processing.

Problem: Some food remains on top of Disc after slicing or shredding.
Solution: This is normal. If desired, cut remaining bits by hand; add to mixture.

RECIPE ADAPTATION: HOW TO DO IT. THINGS TO LOOK FOR.

Once you learn how to use the Food Processor, you can read any recipe from your own file, cookbooks or magazines with food processing in mind. Ask yourself, how can the Food Processor help with this recipe? It can mince, chop, shred and slice. If the recipe calls for dicing, could you slice or coarsely chop the food instead?

To save clean-up, most of the recipes in this cookbook have been written with ingredients in the order of processing rather than use. You can rearrange any recipe

the same way. The chart on the next page will help you with quantities. However, the Food Processor may intensify the flavor of some ingredients, like onion, so unless you are partial to those flavors, use a little less the first time.

Look through your favorite recipes. The Food Processor can help speed preparation of many of them. Notations with the Meatloaf recipe below, show how simple it is to adapt a recipe. After you've tried this with some favorite recipes, you'll be able to do it easily.

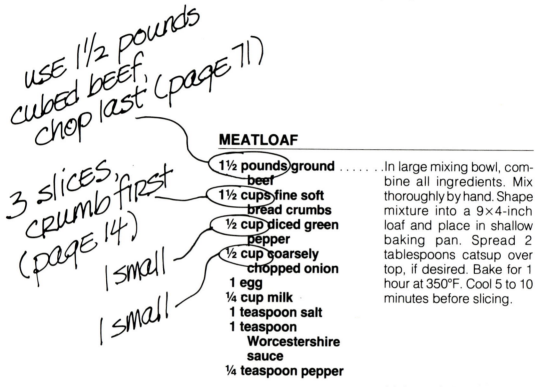

use 1½ pounds cubed beef, chop last (page 71)

3 slices, crumb first (page 14)

1 small

1 small

MEATLOAF

1½ **pounds ground beef**
1½ **cups fine soft bread crumbs**
½ **cup diced green pepper**
½ **cup coarsely chopped onion**
1 **egg**
¼ **cup milk**
1 **teaspoon salt**
1 **teaspoon Worcestershire sauce**
¼ **teaspoon pepper**

In large mixing bowl, combine all ingredients. Mix thoroughly by hand. Shape mixture into a 9×4-inch loaf and place in shallow baking pan. Spread 2 tablespoons catsup over top, if desired. Bake for 1 hour at 350°F. Cool 5 to 10 minutes before slicing.

Makes 6 (1-inch) servings

See Quick 'N Easy Meatloaf, page 71, for this same recipe with complete processing directions.

TABLE OF SUBSTITUTIONS

For your convenience, the list below provides you with some common food substitutions. If you don't have the food listed in the "To Replace" column, substitute with the food opposite.

TO REPLACE: **USE:**

Bouillon cube:
  1 chicken or beef . . . . 1 teaspoon granules
Garlic:
  1 small clove, peeled . . . . ⅛ teaspoon powder

Herbs:
  1 teaspoon fresh . . . . about ½ teaspoon dried
Ice cubes:
  1 standard-size (2×1-in.) . . . . 2 small (1×1-in.)
Lemon:
  Juice of 1 fresh . . . . . 2 to 3 tablespoons reconstituted
Mushrooms:
  ½ lb. fresh . . . . 1 can (6-oz.)
Mustard:
  1 teaspoon dry . . . . 1 tablespoon prepared
Tomatoes:
  1 can (16-oz.) . . . . 2 cups fresh, chopped

TABLE OF EQUIVALENTS

Here is a chart of some frequently used foods. Refer to this list to determine the total amount of an ingredient you will need to equal the chopped, sliced or shredded amount called for in a recipe.

PROCESS: **TO MAKE ABOUT:**

Apple: 1 medium,
   coarsely chopped or sliced ....1 cup
Banana: 1 small, mashed ....½ cup
Bread: (3½-in. sq.), 1 slice fresh, crumbed .....½ cup
Bread: (3½-in. sq.), 1 slice dry, crumbed ......⅓ cup
Cabbage: ½ medium head,
   (1 lb., 5 to 6½-in. dia.), sliced ....6 cups
Carrots: 1 medium,
   chopped, shredded, sliced ....1 cup
Chicken: 1 breast, cooked, cubed ....1 cup
Celery: 1 medium stalk,
   coarsely chopped or sliced ....½ cup
Cheese: 4 oz. Cheddar, shredded ......1 to 1½ cups
Cheese: 4 oz. Swiss, shredded ....1 cup
Cheese: 1 oz. Parmesan, grated ....¼ cup

Cucumber: 1 medium (6×1½-in.), shredded ...1 cup
Cucumber: 1 medium (6×1½-in.), sliced ....1½ cups
Ice cubes: 1 large (2×1½-in.) ....⅓ cup
Mushrooms: 4 oz. fresh,
   chopped or sliced ....1¼ cups
Pepper, green: ½ medium, chopped ....½ cup
Potatoes: 1 medium, chopped or sliced ....¾ cup
Potatoes: 1 medium, shredded ....½ cup
Onions: 1 small (1½ to 2-in. dia.),
   coarsely chopped or sliced ....½ cup
Onions: 1 medium (2½ to 3-in. dia.),
   coarsely chopped or sliced ....1 cup
Onions: 1 large (3½ to 4-in. dia.),
   coarsely chopped or sliced ....2 cups
Onions: 1 medium green, chopped .....1 tablespoon
Parsley, fresh: 4 to 5 sprigs
   (leaves only), chopped ....1 tablespoon
Tomatoes: 4 medium (1 lb.),
   chopped or sliced ....3 cups
Tomatoes: 1 medium (2½-in. dia.),
   chopped or sliced ....¾ cup

POINTS TO REMEMBER ABOUT FOOD PROCESSING

Be sure to read the Use and Care Book which is packed with your GE Food Processor plus Blender. It contains important information for correct use and care for this appliance. Following is a summary of some important points to remember:

SAFETY

Read Use and Care Book for all safety information.

To avoid injury, never put Knife Blade, Reversible Disc or Blender Blades on base without first having put Food Processor Bowl or Blender Jar in place properly.

Always operate processor with cover correctly in place and Blender with Jar correctly locked into place. Do not attempt to defeat the interlock systems.

Handle the Knife Blade, Reversible Disc and Blender Blades carefully to avoid cuts. Grasp the Knife Blade by the hub and always remove it before removing processed food from the Bowl.

Never feed food into the food chute by hand when slicing or shredding. Always use the food pusher.

Keep hands and utensils out of Bowl or Blender Jar while operating to prevent personal injury or damage to the appliance.

After turning Blender on with hot liquid in the Jar, immediately remove center insert of the two-piece lid to prevent buildup of steam inside the Jar.

Never exceed Fill Level on Bowl or 4½ cups liquid in Blender Jar.

Make sure motor and Disc, Knife Blade or Blender Blades have stopped before removing processor cover or blender lid.

Always use push button controls on base to operate the appliance. Never use the cover release knob to turn processor off or unlock Blender Jar to turn Blender off. This would allow appliance to turn on unexpectedly when cover or Jar was again locked in place.

USE

Process or blend foods only in the quantities indicated or as specified in the recipes. If you want a larger amount or want to double a recipe, prepare a second batch.

Prepare recipes using the appliance recommended. Do not prepare Blender recipes in the Food Processor since liquid amounts may overflow the processor Bowl.

Timing is very important with the Food Processor or Blender. Overprocessing can happen quickly. Use the Pulse button often when chopping, and check the food between each Pulse. A clock with a second hand will be most helpful when following recipes in this book, or you may count seconds as 1001, 1002, etc.

If you own a GE Food Processor, Model FP1, the Blender recipes in this book may be prepared in another household blender, although times and results may not be the same.

If your Food Processor is not a GE, techniques for using it will be different and you may not get the same results. However, you will find the book useful and informative.

49

Taste-Tempting
Appetizers

Surprise your family with an appetizer before dinner and make an event of a simple family meal. Provide a regal array for an important party. The Food Processor makes the pâtés, the dips, and the fillings.

Many of these recipes can be prepared in advance, so you can relax and enjoy the party with your guests. If you're serving a crowd, make successive batches of a favorite food, or single batches of an impressive variety. To cap it all, try at least one hot appetizer. All it takes is a little last minute baking or reheating.

1. Curry Vegetable Dip, page 52
2. Cheese Straws, page 55
3. Processor Sliced Cucumbers, page 28
4. Deviled Eggs, page 55
5. Vegetables with Cheesy Olive Ball Stuffing, page 54
6. Cheddar Cheese Pennies, page 55

HOT AND SPICY TACO DIP ∾

1 small clove garlic, peeled **1 medium onion,** quartered	Position **Knife Blade** in **Bowl.** Drop garlic through food chute with Processor running. Turn off. Add onion. Pulse until finely chopped, about 5 seconds.
1 tablespoon vegetable oil **1 pound ground beef** (page 71)	In 12-inch skillet, heat oil over medium-high heat. Cook onion and beef until meat loses its redness.
½ green pepper, cut in 6 pieces	Position **Knife Blade** in **Bowl.** Add pepper; Pulse until coarsely chopped; add to meat and continue cooking.
1 can (15- to 20-oz.) red kidney beans, undrained	Position **Knife Blade** in **Bowl;** add kidney beans. Process until beans are smooth, about 5 seconds.
½ cup catsup **1 to 3 teaspoons** chili powder **1 teaspoon salt** **¼ teaspoon pepper**	Stir beans, catsup and seasonings into meat. Reduce heat and simmer 10 minutes. To serve, place in chafing dish or electic skillet; sprinkle with a little shredded cheese and sliced olives, if desired. Serve with corn chips.

Makes 3 to 3½ cups

NOTE: Dip can be prepared ahead; cover and refrigerate. At serving time, add a small amount of catsup; reheat and garnish with cheese and olives.

GUACAMOLE ∾

A spicy Mexican avocado dip

1 large avocado, peeled, halved, pitted, cut in 1-inch pieces **¼ cup mayonnaise** **1½ tablespoons instant** minced onion **1 tablespoon lemon** juice **½ teaspoon salt** **¼ to ½ teaspoon** chili powder **¼ teaspoon pepper**	Position **Knife Blade** in **Bowl;** add all ingredients. Pulse 2 or 3 times to mix; then process for 1 minute. (It may be necessary to stop and scrape down sides of **Bowl** once or twice during processing.) Refrigerate until serving time. Serve with corn chips or crackers.

Makes about 1 cup

CURRY VEGETABLE DIP ∾

1 package (8-oz.) cream cheese, chilled, cut in 6 pieces **½ cup sour cream** **¼ cup raisins** **½ teaspoon curry** powder **¼ teaspoon salt**	Position **Knife Blade** in **Bowl;** add all ingredients. Pulse to mix, about 40 seconds. Refrigerate until serving time. Serve with bite-size pieces of raw vegetables or crackers.

Makes 1½ cups

LO-CAL CHEESE DIP ∾

2 cups creamed cottage cheese **2 teaspoons instant** beef bouillon granules **2 teaspoons instant** minced onion **2 teaspoons lemon** juice	Position **Knife Blade** in **Bowl;** add all ingredients. Process until smooth, about 1 minute. Serve with raw vegetables or crackers.

Makes 2 cups

VARIATION:
Shred ½ unpeeled cucumber; place in strainer to drain. Process cheese dip, substituting 1 teaspoon dill weed or dill seed for beef bouillon. Add cucumber; process 5 seconds more.

ONION-TUNA PÂTÉ ∾

1 can (6½- to 7-oz.) tuna, drained **1 package (3-oz.)** cream cheese, chilled, cut in 3 pieces **1 small onion,** quartered **1 medium dill pickle,** quartered **½ teaspoon prepared** horseradish **Dash cayenne pepper**	Position **Knife Blade** in **Bowl;** add all ingredients. Process until mixed and ingredients are finely chopped, about 25 seconds. (May be necessary to stir mixture once or twice.) Pack into 2- to 3-cup crock or small bowl. Cover; refrigerate until serving. Serve with crackers, melba toast or celery sticks.

Makes 1¾ cups

PARTY CHEESE SPREAD ∾

1 package (10-oz.) sharp Cheddar cold pack cheese food, cut in 10 pieces **½ cup sour cream** **2 tablespoons sherry**	Position **Knife Blade** in **Bowl;** add all ingredients. Process until smooth, about 15 seconds. Serve with assorted crackers and raw vegetables. Store leftover spread in refrigerator.

Makes 1½ cups

PET

Just

8

3

on
7-
ver
and
until
pok-
(Do
s will
thly.)

de in
s and
Add to
ninutes
m heat.

lade in
mixture
ueur and
cess for
top and
es of **Bowl.**
onds more.

small bowl.
ore serving,
atula. Invert
y, if desired.

on serving ...
Reshape mold slightly if necess...

Makes 1 (¾-cup) pâté

CHICKEN LIVER PÂTÉ

1 pound chicken livers **¼ cup butter or margarine**	Clean and dry livers on paper towel. Cut into smaller pieces. In 10-inch skillet sauté livers in melted butter until they lose their pink color. Stir occasionally.
1 small clove garlic, peeled **1 small onion, halved** **1 apple, peeled, quartered, cored (page 18)**	Position **Knife Blade** in **Bowl.** Drop garlic through food chute with Processor running. Add onion and apple. Pulse to chop coarsely. Add apple mixture to livers; cook about 5 minutes. Place mixture in **Blender Jar.**
½ cup light cream **1 tablespoon lemon juice** **1 teaspoon salt** **Dash each allspice, cloves, nutmeg, pepper**	Pour cream into skillet; stir to combine with pan juices. Pour over livers. Add seasonings. Process at Blend speed until smooth, about 1 minute. (It may be necessary to stop and stir once or twice during blending.)

Pour into 2-cup crock or serving dish. Cover pâté with plastic wrap and refrigerate. Serve with assorted crackers.

Makes 2 cups

HOW TO MAKE A MOLDED PETITE PÂTÉ

Prepare and cook chicken livers and onions as directed in the recipe. Position Knife Blade in Bowl.

Add liver mixture, liqueur and seasonings. Process 20 seconds, scraping down Bowl after 10 seconds. Pack in oiled mold and refrigerate.

Loosen pâté from mold with spatula. Turn out on serving plate. Reshape mold with spatula, if necessary.

Cheesy Olive Ball

SIMPLE SNOW CAPPED PÂTÉ ❧

Pâté:

1 small clove garlic, peeled	Position **Knife Blade** in **Bowl.** Drop garlic through food chute with Processor running and mince. Turn off. Add liverwurst, basil and instant onion. Process 10 seconds. Stop and scrape down sides of **Bowl.** Process 10 more seconds. Press mixture into 2-cup mold or small dish. Chill in refrigerator several hours or overnight. Unmold pâté by running small metal spatula around edge and invert onto serving plate.
1 package (8-oz.) **liverwurst, cut in** **8 pieces**	
½ teaspoon each basil, **instant minced** **onion**	

Topping:

1 small clove garlic, peeled	Position **Knife Blade** in **Bowl.** Drop garlic through food chute with Processor running and mince. Turn off. Add remaining ingredients. Process 5 seconds. Stop and scrape down sides; process 5 seconds more. Frost top and sides of mold. Chill until serving.
1 package (3-oz.) **cream cheese,** **chilled, cut in** **3 pieces**	
1 teaspoon **mayonnaise** **Dash hot pepper** **sauce**	

Makes 1 (8-ounce) pâté

CHEESY OLIVE BALL ❧

8 sprigs parsley **(page 37) or ½ cup** **nuts**	Position **Knife Blade** in **Bowl.** Pulse until parsley (or nuts) is finely chopped, about 10 to 15 seconds. Transfer to sheet of wax paper and cover.
1 package (8-oz.) **cream cheese,** **chilled, cut in** **6 pieces** **⅓ cup stuffed green** **olives, well drained** **½ teaspoon seasoned** **salt** **⅛ to ¼ teaspoon garlic** **or onion powder**	Position **Knife Blade** in **Bowl.** Add remaining ingredients. Pulse to mix, about 60 seconds. It may be necessary to stop and stir mixture once or twice. Turn mixture out onto wax paper; mound into ball, gathering wax paper around it.

Place in freezer until firm, but not frozen, about 45 minutes. Remove wax paper and roll cheese ball in chopped parsley. Shape into round ball. Wrap in wax paper and refrigerate until serving time. Serve with crackers or raw vegetable sticks.

Makes 1 (8-ounce) ball

BLUE CHEESE BALL ❧

½ cup walnuts	Position **Knife Blade** in **Bowl;** add nuts. Pulse to chop coarsely; set aside in small bowl.
8 ounces blue cheese, **chilled, cut in** **1-inch cubes** **1 package (8-oz.)** **cream cheese,** **softened, cut in** **6 pieces** **½ cup walnuts**	Position **Knife Blade** in **Bowl.** Drop blue cheese cubes through food chute with Processor running. Add cream cheese and nuts.

Process until mixture is smooth, about 40 seconds. (It may be necessary to stop and scrape down sides of **Bowl** once or twice.) Spoon cheese mixture onto sheet of wax paper. Wrap and chill in refrigerator for at least 2 hours. Spread reserved nuts on sheet of wax paper. Shape cheese mixture into ball and roll in nuts. Store in refrigerator until serving time. Serve with assorted crackers or celery.

Makes 1 (16-ounce) cheese ball

f, lengthwise,
olks. Position
n **Bowl.** Add
e whites. Add
 chili sauce,
stard and salt
se until mixed
 about 20 sec-
g white halves.
h olive slices,
aprika, if desir-
rate until serv-

Makes 1 dozen

Knife Blade in
 Disc above it,
g side up; shred

Disc. Add flour,
ng, caraway seeds
to **Bowl.** Pulse un-
ening and cheese
nto flour, about 20
s.

seeds
½ teaspoon salt

3 tablespoons cold . . . . .Add water, all at once,
water   through food chute with
                        Processor running. Pro-
                        cess about 10 seconds.

Preheat oven to 400°F. Press dough into a ball. Roll out
on floured surface to a 15×12-inch rectangle. Sprinkle
lightly with salt. Cut into 4×1-inch strips. Place on ungreased cookie sheet. Bake until lightly browned, 8 to 10
minutes.

Makes 48 appetizers

CHEDDAR CHEESE PENNIES

8 ounces Cheddar	Position **Knife Blade** in
cheese, chilled, cut	**Bowl** with **Disc** above it,
to fit food chute	**shredding side up;** shred
	cheese.
1 cup all-purpose	Remove **Disc.** Add remain-
flour	ing ingredients to **Bowl.**
½ **cup soft butter**	Process until mixture forms
or margarine	a ball, about 10 seconds.
1 teaspoon dry	
mustard	

Preheat oven to 400°F. Roll dough into 1-inch balls and
place 2 inches apart on ungreased cookie sheets. Bake
for 12 to 15 minutes. Serve warm.

Makes 36 appetizers

TANGY STUFFED MUSHROOMS

8 ounces fresh	Wash mushrooms; careful-
mushrooms, small	ly remove stems and set
or medium	aside. Drain caps, hollow
1 small onion,	side down, on paper towels.
quartered	Position **Knife Blade** in
¼ **cup butter or**	**Bowl.** Add mushroom
margarine	stems and onion; Pulse to
	chop finely. In 10-inch skil-
	let melt butter and sauté
	onion mixture.
1 slice fresh bread, ...	Preheat oven to 350°F. Po-
white or whole	sition **Knife Blade** in **Bowl.**
wheat, broken in	Add bread and blue
4 pieces	cheese. Pulse until finely
1 ounce blue cheese,	crumbled. Combine bread,
chilled, about 2	blue cheese and salt with
1-inch squares	mixture in skillet.
½ **teaspoon salt**	

Fill mushroom caps, pressing mixture into hollows. Place
in shallow baking dish. Bake for 10 to 12 minutes. Serve
hot. Garnish with chopped parsley just before serving, if
desired.

Makes 14 to 20 (depending on size)

NOTE: May be stuffed in advance. Refrigerate until
ready to bake.

Simple Snow Capped Pâté

Antipasto Vegetables

ANTIPASTO VEGETABLES

Arrange Antipasto on individual plates and serve as appetizer or salad.

2 large carrots, peeled . . .Position **Disc** in **Bowl** with
1 small green pepper, **slicing side up.** Slice as
  halved directed on pages 23 to 39.
2 medium stalks When sliced vegetables
  celery, each cut reach Fill Level, empty into
  crosswise in thirds large mixing bowl.
1 small sweet onion
½ small cauliflower,
  cut into flowerets

1 cup white wine . . . . .In 10-inch skillet combine
  vinegar vinegar, oil, water, sugar
⅓ cup olive oil and seasonings. Add slic-
¼ cup water ed vegetables and care-
2 tablespoons sugar fully stir to coat. Bring to a
1 teaspoon salt boil. Reduce heat and sim-
½ teaspoon oregano mer until slightly tender,
½ teaspoon tarragon about 4 to 5 minutes.

1 jar (2-oz.) chopped . . . . .Add pimiento. Transfer to
  pimiento, drained storage container and
 cover. Refrigerate at least
 24 hours. Drain well; serve
 cold.

 Makes 8 (½-cup) servings

STEAK TARTARE

A freshly chopped beef appetizer served uncooked

1 pound lean, tender . . . .Position **Knife Blade** in
  beef, with fat and **Bowl;** add 1 cup beef and
  gristle removed, part of onions, anchovies
  cut in 1-inch cubes and parsley. Pulse to chop
6 green onions, cut in evenly, about 10 seconds.
  1-inch pieces, or 1 Place in mixing bowl. Re-
  small onion, peat with remaining beef,
  quartered onions, anchovies and
3 anchovies parsley.
2 sprigs parsley

1 egg or egg yolk . . . . . . .Add remaining ingredients
½ teaspoon salt to mixing bowl. Stir well
½ teaspoon with fork to mix egg and
  Worcestershire seasonings in meat. Shape
  sauce into ball. Refrigerate until
⅛ teaspoon pepper ready to serve. Serve with
 crackers or thinly sliced
 dark bread.

 Makes about 1 pound ball

COCKTAIL HAMBURGERS

1 slice fresh bread, ...Position **Knife Blade** in
  white or whole **Bowl.** Add bread and on-
  wheat, broken in ion. Process until finely
  4 pieces chopped.
1 small onion,
  quartered

1 pound ground beef . . . .Combine bread and onion
  (page 71) with remaining ingredients;
2 tablespoons milk mix well. Shape into ½-inch
½ teaspoon salt balls; flatten to ½-inch thick.
  Dash pepper

1 tablespoon . . . . .In large skillet heat oil over
  vegetable oil medium high heat.

Brown on both sides. Drain off fat when necessary. Serve
with Barbecue Sauce (below) if desired.

Makes 4½ dozen bite-size appetizers

BARBECUE SAUCE

1 small onion, halved . . . .Add all ingredients to
¼ small green pepper, **Blender Jar.** Cover and
  cut in thirds blend at Puree speed until
¾ cup catsup or smooth, about 15 seconds.
  chili sauce Pour into 1-quart sauce-
¼ cup water pan; cover and simmer 30
1 tablespoon brown minutes. Use as a dip for
  sugar Cocktail Hamburgers
1 tablespoon lemon (above) or as a sauce for
  juice other beef recipes.
1 teaspoon
  Worcestershire
  sauce
  Dash pepper

Makes 1¼ cups

Flavorful
Soups

Pictured on previous page: Cioppino Soup

A soup can be many things: the start of a formal dinner, the main dish for a hearty family supper, a warming lunch on a cool day, or a refreshing cooler on a hot one. Delicious soups are easy to make; the hardest part is chopping, slicing or puréeing good things that combine to give them flavor. Let the Food Processor do that work for you.

MAKE-YOUR-OWN MINESTRONE 🖚 🌙

Minestrone means "big soup" and every region of Italy has its own variation. Substitute any vegetable in season.

1 small clove garlic, ...Position **Knife Blade** in dry
peeled Bowl; drop garlic through
1 medium onion, food chute with Processor
quartered running. Then add onion
3 sprigs parsley and parsley. Pulse to chop finely.

¼ cup olive or . . . . .In 8-quart pot heat oil over
vegetable oil medium heat. Add onion
6 cups water mixture and sauté until soft.
2 tablespoons instant Add water and bouillon.
beef bouillon
granules

2 medium potatoes, ...Position **Knife Blade** in
peeled, quartered Bowl; add potatoes. Pulse
2 cups (½ lb.) green to chop coarsely. Add to
beans, cut in soup. Repeat with green
1-inch pieces beans, then tomatoes.
4 medium tomatoes,*
peeled, quartered

2 medium stalks . . . . .Position **Disc** in **Bowl** with
celery, each cut **slicing side up;** slice cel-
crosswise in thirds ery and carrots; add to
2 medium carrots, soup. Cover soup and sim-
peeled, halved mer over medium-low heat,
crosswise 45 minutes.

1 can (15¼- to 20-oz.) . . . .Add beans and macaroni;
kidney beans, boil until macaroni is ten-
undrained der, about 15 minutes.
½ cup elbow or other Serve topped with grated
macaroni Parmesan cheese (page 14), if desired.

Makes 10 (1-cup) servings

*1 can (16-oz.) whole tomatoes may be substituted for fresh tomatoes.

CIOPPINO 🖚

A famous fish soup from San Francisco. Delicious with crusty bread.

¼ cup olive or . . . . .In 4-quart saucepan heat
vegetable oil oil over medium heat.

½ cup parsley leaves . . . .Position dry **Knife Blade**
2 or 3 cloves garlic, in dry **Bowl**; add parsley.
peeled Process to chop coarsely;
add garlic through food
chute with Processor run-
ning. Add to oil and sauté.

1 medium onion, ...Position **Knife Blade** in
quartered **Bowl**; add onion and green
½ medium green pepper. Pulse to chop
pepper, cut in coarsely, 2 to 3 seconds.
6 pieces Add to oil and sauté vegetables about 10 minutes,
stirring occasionally.

1 can (28-oz.) . . . . .Stir in tomatoes, tomato
tomatoes, sauce, water, wine and
undrained seasonings. Cover and
1 can (8-oz.) tomato simmer over medium-low
sauce heat, 30 minutes.
2 cups water
½ cup dry sherry or
white wine
1 tablespoon sugar
2 teaspoons salt
¼ teaspoon marjoram
¼ teaspoon oregano
¼ teaspoon pepper

1 dozen fresh . . . . .If using fresh littleneck
littleneck clams,* clams, add to soup and
or 1 can (6½- to simmer 15 to 20 minutes
10-oz.) clams, or until shells pop open.
undrained Then add remaining fish
2 pounds fresh or and cook 5 minutes longer.
frozen, boned If canned clams are used,
white fish, cut in add all fish at once. Cover
pieces and simmer 5 minutes. Salt
½ to 1 pound raw, to taste.
cleaned shrimp or
rock lobster tails,
cut in 1-inch pieces,
including shell
Salt

Makes 8 (1½-cup) servings

*To clean live clams, scrub shells; let stand in salted water 15 minutes. Drain and repeat process.

EASY FRENCH ONION SOUP 🌀

4 tablespoons butter	In 4-quart pot melt butter over moderate heat.
7 medium onions, halved lengthwise	Position **Disc** in **Bowl** with **slicing side up;** slice onions. When onions reach Fill Level, empty into pot. Sauté until soft.
3 cans (10½-oz.) condensed beef broth **3 cups water** **3 whole peppercorns**	Add beef broth, water and peppercorns. Bring to a boil; reduce heat. Cover and simmer for 10 minutes.
½ cup full bodied red wine	Stir in wine and serve.

Makes 10 (1-cup) servings

NOTE: If desired, top each serving with a piece of toasted French bread and sprinkle with fresh Parmesan cheese, grated in the Processor. Soup may be set under a preheated broiler for a moment or two to brown cheese.

CLAM CHOWDER NEW ENGLAND STYLE 〰️🌀

3 slices bacon	In 3-quart saucepan fry bacon until crisp. Remove and crumble bacon; leave 2 tablespoons fat in pan.
1 small onion, quartered **1 medium stalk celery, cut in 1-inch pieces**	Position **Knife Blade** in **Bowl;** add onion and celery. Pulse to chop finely. Add to pan; sauté until soft. Remove pan from heat.
1 carrot, peeled, cut 1-inch pieces	Position **Knife Blade** in **Bowl;** add carrot. Pulse to chop coarsely. Add to pan.
1 medium potato, peeled, quartered **½ cup water**	Position **Disc** in **Bowl** with **slicing side up;** slice potato. Add water, bacon and potatoes to pan; cover. Cook over medium heat until vegetables are tender, 15 to 20 minutes. Stir occasionally. Add ¼ cup more water if necessary.
1 can (6½- to 8-oz.) minced clams, undrained **2 tablespoons butter*, melted** **3 tablespoons all-purpose flour*** **2 cups milk** **½ teaspoon salt Dash pepper**	Stir in clams. Combine butter and flour, making a smooth paste. Add to soup; then add milk, salt and pepper. Cook over low heat, stirring constantly, until soup thickens, about 2 minutes.

Makes about 4 (1-cup) servings

*For a thin broth-like chowder, do not add butter or flour.

Easy French Onion Soup

GAZPACHO SOUP 🝫

A cold Spanish soup — thick and spicy.

4 cups tomato juice, divided **2 tablespoons olive or vegetable oil** **2 tablespoons wine vinegar** **1½ teaspoons salt Dash pepper** **4 medium tomatoes, peeled, quartered** **1 small sweet onion, quartered** **½ medium green pepper, cut in 6 pieces** **½ medium cucumber, halved lengthwise, cut in 1-inch pieces** **1 medium stalk celery, cut in 1-inch pieces**	Add 2 cups tomato juice, olive oil, vinegar, salt, pepper and about half the vegetables to **Blender Jar.** Do not exceed the 4½ cup marking on side of **Jar.** Cover and blend at Liquefy speed for 1 minute. Pour into large pitcher. Repeat with remaining tomato juice and vegetables. Add to pitcher and stir well. Cover and chill thoroughly before serving. Garnish with seasoned croutons, if desired.

Makes 8 (1-cup) servings

CREAMY CHICKEN SOUP 🌑 ⌒

1 (2- to 2½-lb.) frying . . . . In 8-quart heavy pot com-
  chicken, cut   bine chicken, water, bouil-
  in pieces   lon and seasonings.
1 quart water
2 tablespoons instant
  chicken bouillon
  granules
1 bay leaf
1 teaspoon salt
½ teaspoon curry
  powder
¼ teaspoon pepper

2 medium carrots, ... Position **Disc** in **Bowl** with
  peeled   **slicing side up.** Slice veg-
1 medium stalk celery,   etables. Add to pot. Cover
  cut crosswise   and simmer until chicken
  in thirds   is tender, about 1 hour. Re-
1 small onion   move chicken and bay leaf.
                              Skim fat from soup, if nec-
                              essary. Bone chicken and
                              cut into cubes. Position
                              Knife Blade in **Bowl.** Add
                              about 1½ cups chicken
                              cubes; Pulse to chop very
                              coarsely, 2 to 3 times. Add
                              to soup and repeat with re-
                              maining chicken.

1 quart milk . . . . Add milk to soup. Bring just
                              to a boil.

6 tablespoons chicken . . . Combine fat and flour to
  fat or butter, melted   make a smooth paste. Stir
½ cup flour   into soup.

Cook slowly, stirring constantly, until slightly thickened.
Season with additional salt and pepper to taste.

Makes 10 (1-cup) servings

LO-CAL VEGETABLE SOUP 🌑

2 carrots, peeled . . . . Position **Disc** in **Bowl** with
2 large celery stalks,   **slicing side up.** Pack car-
  including leaves,   rots and celery upright in
  each cut crosswise   food chute together. Slice.
  in thirds   Then slice onion and cab-
1 medium onion,   bage. When vegetables
  halved   reach Fill Level, transfer to
¼ small head cabbage,   3-quart saucepan, and
  cut in wedges   slice remaining vegetables.

2 cups (1-lb. can) . . . . . . Add juice, water, bouillon
  tomato juice   and seasonings to sauce-
2 cups water   pan. Bring to full boil; cov-
2 tablespoons instant   er, then simmer 1 hour.
  beef bouillon   One cup of this tasty soup
  granules   equals about 65 calories.
½ teaspoon each of
  oregano, thyme,
  basil

Makes 5 (1-cup) servings

HEARTY SOUP SPECIAL 🌑

3 large stalks celery, ... Position **Disc** in **Bowl** with
  each cut in thirds   **slicing side up.** Slice cel-
3 potatoes, peeled   ery, potatoes, carrots and
2 carrots, peeled   onions. Empty **Bowl** as
2 onions, halved   vegetables reach Fill Level.

2 cans (10¾-oz.) . . . . In 8-quart heavy pot, com-
  condensed chicken   bine soup, celery, potatoes,
  broth   carrots, onions, bay leaf
1 bay leaf   and thyme. Add water.
1 teaspoon thyme   Simmer for 15 minutes.
2 cups water

2 small zucchini or . . . . . Position **Disc** in **Bowl** with
  8 ounces fresh   **slicing side up.** Slice zuc-
  mushrooms   chini. Add to soup with re-
4 cups diced, cooked   maining ingredients, sim-
  chicken   mer another 30 minutes.
1 can (20-oz.) chick   Add more water if neces-
  peas, undrained or   sary. Stir occasionally.
  1 can (12-oz.) corn,
  undrained
1 package (10-oz.)
  frozen pea pods,
  string beans or
  lima beans
¼ to ½ cup rice or
  pasta

Makes about 8 (2-cup) servings

VICHYSSOISE 🌑 ⌴

A rich, cold potato soup from France.

1 tablespoon butter . . . . . In 2-quart saucepan melt
  or margarine   butter. Position **Disc** in
1 medium onion, cut   **Bowl** with **slicing side up.**
  to fit food chute   Slice onion. Add to sauce-
                              pan and sauté until soft,
                              about 3 minutes.

4 small potatoes, ... Position **Disc** in **Bowl** with
  peeled   **slicing side up.** Slice po-
1 can (10¾-oz.)   tatoes. Add potatoes,
  condensed   chicken broth, water, salt
  chicken broth   and pepper to saucepan.
½ cup water   Reduce heat to simmer
½ teaspoon salt   temperature; cover and
⅛ teaspoon pepper   simmer until potatoes are
                              done, about 15 minutes.

1½ cups half and half . . . Pour potato mixture into
                              Blender Jar. Add half and
                              half and cover. Blend at
                              Blend speed 20 to 30 sec-
                              onds. Refrigerate until thor-
                              oughly chilled, about 4
                              hours.

Makes 5 (1-cup) servings

Satisfying
Sandwiches

Sandwiches are another processor specialty. Just look at the variety offered here. A sandwich spread and a tray of crackers make a tasty appetizer, too. Create your own combinations with leftover meat and experiment with seasonings, such as curry, chili, cumin, tarragon or seasoned salts.

TEMPTING TACOS 🍽️〰️🎱

¼ to ½ small head iceberg lettuce	Position **Disc** in **Bowl** with **slicing side up;** slice lettuce. If lettuce reaches Fill Level, empty into large mixing bowl and slice remaining lettuce.
2 to 3 medium tomatoes, quartered	Position **Knife Blade** in **Bowl.** Pulse to chop tomatoes, 3 to 4 seconds. Place in small mixing bowl.
1 small clove garlic, peeled 1 small onion, quartered 1 pound ground beef (page 71)	Position **Knife Blade** in **Bowl.** Drop garlic through food chute with Processor running. Turn off. Add onion. Pulse to chop finely. In 10-inch skillet brown beef with onion and garlic; drain off fat.
1 to 1½ teaspoons chili powder ½ teaspoon salt ½ cup catsup	Stir in chili powder and salt, then catsup. Reduce heat and keep warm.
3 to 4 ounces natural Cheddar cheese	Position **Disc** in **Bowl** with **shredding side up;** shred cheese. Put cheese in second small mixing bowl.
18 4½-inch canned tortillas* or 12 6-inch frozen tortillas	Fry tortillas and shape into tacos as directed on package label.
1 jar (8-oz.) taco sauce	Place tacos on serving tray and divide ingredients among them, filling each with a layer of meat mixture, tomatoes, lettuce and cheese. Drizzle with taco sauce.

Makes 12 to 18 tacos

*Leftover tortillas can be stored in refrigerator or frozen.

Top to Bottom: Crunchy Cheese Sandwiches, Tempting Tacos, Short-Cut Pizzas

CRUNCHY CHEESE SANDWICHES ⟿ ❾ ⬤

1 small onion, quartered	Position **Knife Blade** in **Bowl**. Add onion and tomato. Pulse to chop coarsely. Place in large mixing bowl.
1 medium tomato, quartered	
1 medium stalk celery, cut crosswise in 3 pieces	Position **Disc** in **Bowl** with **slicing side up.** Pack chute with celery and green pepper pieces. Slice and add to mixing bowl.
1 small green pepper, quartered	
4 ounces natural Cheddar or Swiss cheese, chilled, cut to fit food chute	Position **Disc** in **Bowl** with **shredding side up;** shred cheese and add to vegetables.
¼ to ½ teaspoon chili powder	Toss mixture with seasonings.
¼ teaspoon salt	
4 slices sandwich bread (any type) Butter	Lightly butter bread. Mound mixture on each slice, spreading to edge of bread. Broil until cheese melts, 4 to 5 minutes. Watch closely. Serve hot.

Makes 4 sandwiches

CHEESE-TOPPED SLOPPY JOES ⟿ ⬤

1 medium onion, quartered	Position **Knife Blade** in **Bowl;** add onion. Pulse to chop coarsely.
1 tablespoon vegetable oil	In 10-inch skillet sauté onion in vegetable oil. Add beef and cook until well browned.
1 pound ground beef	
1 tablespoon all-purpose flour	Reduce heat and stir in flour, oregano and salt. Add tomato sauce; stir until mixture thickens slightly.
½ teaspoon oregano	
¼ teaspoon salt	
1 can (15-oz.) tomato sauce	
4 ounces Cheddar cheese	Position **Disc** in **Bowl** with **shredding side up.** Shred cheese and leave in **Bowl.**
1 loaf French-style bread, about 15-inches long	Cut bread in half crosswise. Then cut each piece in half lengthwise.

Position bread, cut side up, on foil-lined cookie sheet. Broil until well browned. Remove from oven. Spread heaping spoonfuls of meat mixture over toasted bread. Top with shredded cheese. Return to oven and broil until cheese melts.

Makes 4 open-face sandwiches

SHORT-CUT PIZZAS ⬤

4 ounces natural Swiss cheese	Position **Disc** in **Bowl** with **shredding side up.** Shred cheese; leave in **Bowl.**
4 English muffins, split Butter	Toast muffin halves under broiler. Butter lightly.
1 can (8-oz.) tomato sauce Oregano Pepperoni slices (page 42)	Spread muffin halves with 1½ tablespoons sauce. Sprinkle with cheese and oregano. Top each muffin with 2 or 3 slices pepperoni. Broil until cheese melts, about 2 to 4 minutes. Watch closely.

Makes 8 pizza muffins

BUBBLING HAM 'N SWISS MUFFINS ⟿ ⬤

½ green pepper, cut in 6 pieces	Position **Knife Blade** in **Bowl;** add vegetables. Pulse to chop coarsely, 3 to 4 seconds. Place in mixing bowl.
1 small onion, quartered	
1 cup cooked ham, cut in 1-inch cubes	Position **Knife Blade** in **Bowl;** add meat. Pulse to chop coarsely and add to vegetables.
8 ounces natural Swiss cheese, cut to fit food chute	Position **Disc** in **Bowl** with **shredding side up;** shred cheese and add to vegetables.
¼ cup mayonnaise Dash salt and pepper	Add mayonnaise and seasonings. Mix well. (Mixture will be dry.)
4 English muffins, split Butter	Lightly butter muffin halves; spread ⅓ to ½ cup filling on each. Broil until hot and bubbly, 4 to 5 minutes, watching closely, or bake in preheated 400°F. oven for 10 minutes.

Makes 8 halves

HAM SALAD SPREAD 〜🍥

2 cups cooked ham, cut in 1-inch cubes	Position **Knife Blade** in **Bowl.** Add ham; Pulse until coarsely chopped, about 7 seconds. Transfer to mixing bowl.
2 medium stalks celery, each cut crosswise in thirds **4 to 5 tablespoons mayonnaise** **2 teaspoons horseradish**	Position **Disc** in **Bowl** with **slicing side up;** slice celery. Add celery, mayonnaise and horseradish to ham. Mix well.

Makes 2¼ cups

OLD-FASHIONED PEANUT BUTTER 〜

2 cups salted peanuts . . . .Position **Knife Blade** in **Bowl;** add peanuts.
(Do not use dry roasted peanuts.) Process until smooth, about 5 to 6 minutes. For a chunky peanut butter, add 2 tablespoons peanuts after mixture is smooth; process a few seconds more. Store peanut butter in refrigerator.

Makes about 1 cup

NOTE: Homemade peanut butter will be thin. It thickens slightly when refrigerated.

TUNA-EGG SANDWICHES 〜🍥🍥

2 eggs, hard-cooked, halved **1 small onion, quartered**	Position **Knife Blade** in **Bowl;** add egg and onion. Pulse to chop coarsely. Transfer to mixing bowl.
1 can (6½- to 7-oz.) tuna, drained, flaked	Return **Knife Blade** to **Bowl.** Add tuna. Pulse until finely chopped; add to mixing bowl.
¼ pound natural Swiss or Cheddar cheese, chilled	Position **Disc** in **Bowl** with **shredding side up.** Shred cheese. Add to mixing bowl.
2 large stalks celery, each cut crosswise in thirds **¼ cup mayonnaise**	Position **Disc** in **Bowl** with **slicing side up;** slice celery. Add celery and mayonnaise to mixing bowl. Toss well.
6 hard rolls, split **Lettuce leaves**	Spread mixture on bottom half of each roll. Cover with lettuce leaves and then with other half of roll.

Makes 6 sandwiches

TIP: When making luncheon sandwiches, chop ingredients separately for interesting texture. For bite-size party sandwiches, chop all ingredients together until they are almost smooth.

HOW TO MAKE PEANUT BUTTER 〜

Position Knife Blade in Bowl. Add up to 2 cups salted peanuts. Do not use dry roasted peanuts.

Process until peanuts form a ball, then begin to liquefy, about 1 to 2 minutes. Stop and scrape down Bowl.

Process again until smooth, about 4 to 6 minutes. Use high quality peanuts for best results.

EGG SALAD FILLING ⌀

1 small stalk celery, cut in 1-inch pieces ¼ green pepper, cut in thirds	Position **Knife Blade** in **Bowl**; add celery and green pepper. Pulse until fine; drain if necessary. Transfer to mixing bowl.
2 eggs, hard-cooked, halved	Position **Knife Blade** in **Bowl**; add eggs. Pulse until medium fine. Add to celery mixture.
1 tablespoon mayonnaise ¼ teaspoon salt Dash curry powder (optional) Dash pepper	Add mayonnaise and seasonings to celery mixture. Stir well.

Makes 1 cup

CHICKEN SALAD FILLING ⌀

1 small dill pickle, cut in pieces	Position **Knife Blade** in **Bowl**. Add pickle; Pulse to chop evenly. Transfer to a mixing bowl.
1 medium stalk celery, cut in 1-inch pieces	Position **Knife Blade** in **Bowl**. Add celery; Pulse to chop evenly. Add to pickles.
1 cup cubed, cooked chicken	Position **Knife Blade** in **Bowl**; add chicken. Pulse until coarsely chopped.
3 tablespoons mayonnaise 1 teaspoon instant minced onion ½ teaspoon salt ¼ to ½ teaspoon dill weed	Combine chicken, mayonnaise and seasonings with pickle mixture. Stir well.

Makes 1¼ cups

CHEESY OLIVE SPREAD ⌀ ⦿

¼ cup sour cream 10 pimiento-stuffed olives, undrained	Position **Knife Blade** in **Bowl**. Add sour cream and olives.
4 ounces Cheddar cheese, chilled	Position **Disc** above **Knife Blade, shredding side up.** Shred cheese. Remove **Disc,** adding any cheese remaining on **Disc** to **Bowl**. Scrape down sides of **Bowl**. Process until cheese mixture is smooth, about 40 seconds.

Makes about 1 cup

PARTY SANDWICH STACK ⌀

For extra special occasions!

1 pullman sandwich loaf, 15-inch long, bakery sliced	Order bread at bakery. Have loaf sliced lengthwise in ½-inch slices. (You will need 7 inside slices. Save top and bottom crust slices for bread crumbs.)
1 recipe Egg Salad Filling* (opposite)	Prepare fillings.
1 recipe Cheesy Olive Spread (opposite) 1 recipe Chicken Salad Filling* (opposite)	
Soft butter or margarine	Trim crusts off each bread slice. Lightly butter bottom slice of bread. Spread with half of one filling.* Top with second slice; butter and spread with half of second filling. Top with third slice; butter and spread with half of third filling. Repeat with 3 additional slices. Top Sandwich Stack with last bread slice.
1 package (8-oz.) cream cheese, chilled, cut in 6 pieces ¼ to ⅓ cup milk	Position **Knife Blade** in **Bowl**. Add 1 package cream cheese. Start Processor. Add ¼ cup milk through food chute. Process until smooth and spreadable. Add a little more milk if necessary. Spread cheese frosting lightly over top and sides of Stack.
1 package (8-oz.) cream cheese, chilled, cut in 6 pieces ¼ to ⅓ cup milk	Make second batch of cheese frosting as above and spread Stack with second layer, swirling frosting slightly for decorative design.
5 sprigs parsley (page 37)	Position dry **Knife Blade** in dry **Bowl**. Add parsley and chop finely. Sprinkle over Stack. Garnish with cucumber twists, if desired. Chill until serving time.

Makes about 16 (¾-inch) slices

*Process ingredients until finely chopped. If fillings are not easily spreadable, mix in 1 to 2 tablespoons mayonnaise.

Party Sandwich Stack made with rye bread

HOW TO CHOP INGREDIENTS FOR CHICKEN SALAD ∽

Position Knife Blade in Bowl. Chop onion and pickle together; then chop celery separately.

Pulse to chop chicken coarsely. Combine with vegetables, mayonnaise and seasonings in a bowl.

Chop ingredients separately when you want to retain their distinct flavor and texture. Chop together for a smoother filling or spread.

Tantalizing
Meats &
Main Dishes

The Food Processor brings new speed and ease to many of your favorite meats and main dishes. It makes it easier for the busy modern cook to prepare classic American and foreign recipes. Many of these old, traditional recipes began as simple peasant fare, painstakingly prepared by cooks who had more time than money.

Over the years, these special dishes acquired a gourmet image because they were difficult or time-consuming to prepare by hand.

Many of these recipes can now be made faster and with less effort using the General Electric Food Processor.

1. Veal Cutlets with Mushrooms over noodles, page 76
2. Meatloaf Roll-Up, page 71
3. Cheesy Meat Pie, page 73

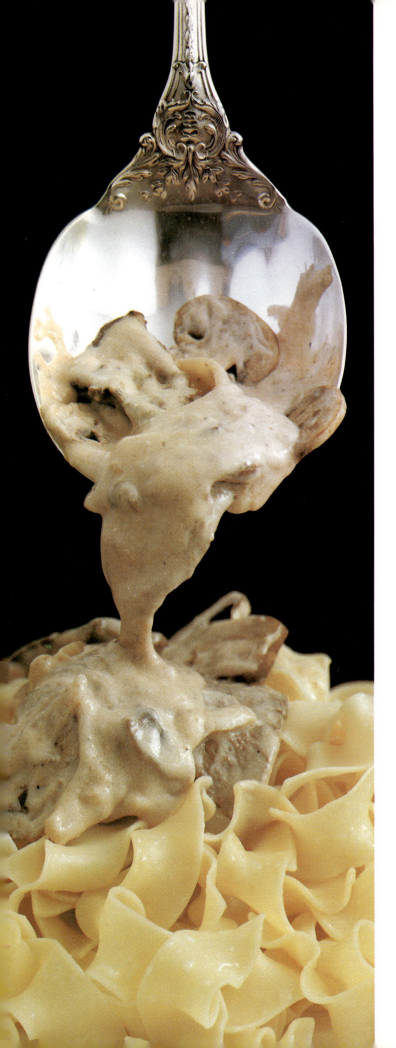

Beef Cubes & Strips

BEEF STROGANOFF

4 ounces fresh mushrooms **1 large onion, halved**	Position **Disc** in **Bowl** with **slicing side up;** slice mushrooms (page 33) and onion.
3 tablespoons vegetable oil	Heat oil in electric skillet over moderate heat, about 350°F. Sauté mushrooms and onion until soft. Remove from skillet and set aside in large dish.
1½ pounds beef round steak, partially frozen (page 30)	Slice meat. Brown about a third of the meat slices at a time in skillet over high heat, about 420°F. (Meat slices brown best when cooked in small quantities.) Drain fat if necessary.
1 cup water **1 tablespoon instant beef bouillon granules** **1 teaspoon dry mustard** **½ teaspoon salt** **⅛ teaspoon pepper**	Reduce heat to simmer temperature, about 200°F. Return vegetables and meat to skillet. Add water and seasonings. Cover, with lid vent closed, and simmer about 45 minutes, or until meat is tender.
2 tablespoons all-purpose flour **¼ cup water**	Combine flour and water and stir until smooth. Stir into meat mixture and cook until sauce thickens, about 2 minutes.
1 cup sour cream	Reduce temperature to low heat, about 150°F. Just before serving, stir in sour cream. Serve over hot noodles.

Makes 4 (¾-cup) servings

Beef Stroganoff

BEEF STEW ⟳

2 tablespoons vegetable oil **4 pounds beef stew meat, cut in 1-inch cubes**	In 8-quart heavy pot, heat oil over medium high heat. Brown meat on all sides, about 12 pieces at a time. (Meat browns better if pieces aren't touching.) Set aside and brown remaining pieces.
1 can (10½-oz.) condensed onion soup **1 cup water** **1 teaspoon salt** **½ teaspoon pepper** **½ teaspoon ground sage**	Reduce heat to simmer. Return meat to skillet and stir in soup, water and seasonings. Cover and simmer for 1½ hours, stirring occasionally.
6 medium carrots, **(pages 12, 16)** **5 medium potatoes, cut to fit food chute** **3 medium onions, halved**	Position **Disc** in **Bowl** with **slicing side up.** Slice vegetables. As vegetables reach Fill Level, empty **Bowl** into pot.

Cover; simmer, stirring occasionally, until meat is tender and vegetables are done, about 40 to 45 minutes.

Makes 8 (1½-cup) servings

HUNGARIAN GOULASH ⟳

3 large onions, halved	Position **Disc** in **Bowl** with **slicing side up.** Slice onions.
3 tablespoons butter or margarine	In 12-inch or electric skillet melt butter. Add onions and sauté until onions are soft, about 5 minutes. Remove onions and place in large mixing bowl.
2 pounds lean stewing beef, cut in 1-inch cubes **1 cup full-bodied red wine or tomato juice** **1 cup water** **1 tablespoon paprika** **2 teaspoons salt** **¼ teaspoon caraway seeds** **¼ teaspoon pepper**	Brown meat on all sides, about 12 pieces at a time. (If meat cubes touch, they will not brown as well.) Reduce heat to simmer temperature. Return meat and onions to skillet. Add wine, water and spices; stir thoroughly. Cover and simmer until meat is tender, about 2 hours. Stir occasionally.
2 tablespoons all-purpose flour **¼ cup water**	Combine flour and water; stir until smooth. Stir into goulash and cook, stirring constantly, until sauce thickens slightly. Garnish with parsley and serve over noodles, if desired.

Makes 4 (1-cup) servings

HOW TO MAKE BEEF STROGANOFF

Slice partially frozen meat. In electric skillet brown at highest heat setting, about 420°F.

Reduce temperature setting to simmer, about 200°F. Cover, with lid vent closed; simmer until meat is tender.

Reduce temperature setting to low heat, about 150°F. Stir in sour cream just before serving. Refer to recipe for complete directions (page 68).

EASY-SLICE SUKIYAKI

1½ pounds beef sirloin, partially frozen (page 30)	Position **Disc** in **Bowl** with **slicing side up;** slice meat and set aside.
1 can (8-oz.) water chestnuts, drained 4 ounces fresh mushrooms 2 medium stalks celery, each cut crosswise in thirds 1 medium onion, quartered ½ head Chinese cabbage, cut to fit food chute	Position **Disc** in **Bowl** with **slicing side up.** Slice each vegetable separately and arrange on tray. Cover and refrigerate until serving time.
1 teaspoon instant beef bouillon granules ⅓ cup hot water ¼ cup soy sauce 1 tablespoon sugar	In 2-cup measure, combine beef granules and water; add soy sauce and sugar. Stir together and set aside.
2 tablespoons vegetable oil	At serving time, heat oil in 12-inch or electric skillet over high heat.

Quickly sear beef on both sides. Add soy mixture and push beef to one side of skillet. Keeping them separate, add water chestnuts, mushrooms, celery and onion. Cook, uncovered, until almost tender, 4 to 5 minutes. Push to side. Add cabbage and cook until heated through, 2 to 3 minutes. Do not overcook. Serve with rice, if desired.

Makes 6 (1-cup) servings

VEGE-BEEF TERIYAKI

1½ pounds lean chuck, 1-inch thick, partially frozen (page 30) ½ cup soy sauce ⅓ cup lemon juice 1 tablespoon brown sugar 2 teaspoons instant minced onion	Position **Disc** in **Bowl** with **slicing side up;** slice meat. Transfer to large mixing bowl. Add soy sauce, lemon juice, brown sugar and instant minced onion to meat. Stir to mix thoroughly. Cover meat and allow to marinate in refrigerator several hours or overnight.
4 ounces fresh mushrooms 1 medium onion, cut to fit food chute 1 small zucchini 1 large stalk celery, cut in 3 pieces ½ medium green pepper	Position **Disc** in **Bowl** with **slicing side up.** Slice vegetables. (For best slicing, fill food chute with zucchini and celery and slice together.) As sliced food reaches Fill Level, empty vegetables into large mixing bowl.
3 tablespoons vegetable oil 1 tablespoon cornstarch 2 tablespoons water	In 12-inch or large electric skillet heat oil over high heat. Add meat pieces only; reserve any liquid.

Stir-fry until lightly browned, about 2 to 3 minutes. Add vegetables and any remaining marinade liquid. Stir-fry until slightly tender, about 1 to 2 minutes. (Vegetables should be crunchy.) In measuring cup, combine cornstarch with water; stir to make a smooth paste. Reduce heat to medium and push meat and vegetables slightly away from one section of skillet. Add cornstarch mixture and stir into liquid in skillet. Cook until liquid thickens slightly. Stir with meat and vegetables. Serve over hot rice, if desired.

Makes 4 (1¼-cup) servings

HOW TO STIR-FRY

Process vegetables and meat as directed in recipe. Have all ingredients ready before cooking. Heat oil in wok or skillet until very hot.

Fry meat, stirring constantly, until almost cooked. Remove, or push to side of skillet. Add vegetables with the longest cooking time.

Stir-fry until almost tender; stir in meat and quick-cooking foods. Do not overcook. Stir-fried dishes should be tender but still crisp.

Ground Beef

HOW TO MAKE CHOPPED RAW BEEF ❧

 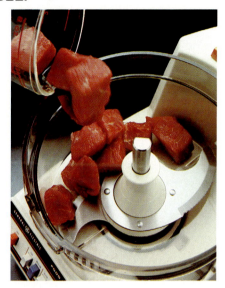 

Trim off gristle and cut meat in 1-inch cubes. For Steak Tartare and lean chopped beef, trim fat. For hamburgers, include some fat for juiciness.

Position Knife Blade in Bowl. Add 1 cup beef cubes. Pulse to chop, checking frequently for desired texture. It takes about 5 to 7 seconds.

Chop meat coarsely for casseroles and hamburgers, finely for Steak Tartare. Repeat with remaining meat.

QUICK 'N EASY MEATLOAF ❧

3 slices fresh whole wheat or white bread, each slice quartered . . . . Preheat oven to 350°F. Position **Knife Blade** in **Bowl.** Add bread; Pulse to chop coarsely, about 7 to 10 seconds.

1 small green pepper, cut in 12 pieces . . . . Position **Knife Blade** in **Bowl;** add green pepper and Pulse to chop coarsely. Add to bread crumbs.

1 small onion, quartered . . . . Position **Knife Blade** in **Bowl.** Add onion. Pulse to chop coarsely. Add to bread crumbs.

1½ pounds ground beef
1 egg
¼ cup milk
1 teaspoon salt
1 teaspoon Worcestershire sauce
¼ teaspoon pepper . . . . . . Add ground beef, egg, milk and seasonings to bread crumbs. Mix thoroughly by hand. Shape meat into a 9×4-inch loaf and place in shallow baking pan. Spread 2 tablespoons catsup over top, if desired. Bake for 1 hour. Cool 5 to 10 minutes before slicing.

Makes 6 (1-inch) servings

MEATLOAF ROLL-UP ❧

3 slices fresh white or whole wheat bread, each slice quartered
1½ pounds ground beef
1 egg
¼ cup milk
1 teaspoon salt
1 teaspoon Worcestershire sauce
¼ teaspoon pepper . . . . . Preheat oven to 350°F. Position **Knife Blade** in **Bowl.** Add bread. Process until crumbed, about 20 seconds. Transfer bread to large mixing bowl. Add beef, egg, milk and seasonings to bread. Mix thoroughly by hand. Transfer beef mixture to sheet of wax paper and roll into a 12×9-inch rectangle.

1 medium green pepper, cut in 12 pieces . . . . Position **Knife Blade** in **Bowl.** Add green pepper. Pulse to chop coarsely. Spread chopped pepper evenly over beef surface.

1 small onion, quartered . . . . Position **Knife Blade** in **Bowl.** Add onion.

Pulse to chop coarsely. Spread chopped onion evenly over beef surface. Roll up, jelly roll fashion, starting with 9-inch side. Use wax paper to help roll. Carefully place meatloaf, seam side down, in shallow baking pan and bake for 1 hour. Cool 5 to 10 minutes before slicing.

Makes 6 (1-inch) servings

Beef 'N Vegetable Pie

GOLD NUGGET MEATLOAF

3 slices fresh bread, any kind, each slice quartered	Preheat oven to 350°F. Position **Knife Blade** in **Bowl.** Pulse to chop coarsely, about 7 to 10 seconds. Transfer to mixing bowl.
2 medium carrots, peeled, cut in 1-inch pieces 1 small onion, quartered	Position **Knife Blade** in **Bowl;** add carrots and onion. Pulse to chop finely, about 10 to 12 seconds. Add to bread crumbs.
1½ pounds ground beef 1 egg ¼ cup milk 1 teaspoon salt 1 teaspoon Worcestershire sauce ¼ teaspoon pepper 2 slices bacon, cut crosswise in half Oregano	Add ground beef, egg, milk and seasonings to bread crumbs. Mix thoroughly by hand. Shape meat into 9×4-inch loaf and place in shallow baking pan. Place bacon slices on top; sprinkle with oregano. Bake for 1 hour. Cool 5 to 10 minutes before slicing.

Makes 6 (1-inch) servings

BEEF 'N VEGETABLE PIE

1 recipe One Crust Butter Pie Crust (page 138)	Prepare pastry dough; set aside. Preheat oven to 350°F.
2 large stalks celery, each cut crosswise in thirds 2 medium potatoes, cut to fit food chute 2 carrots, peeled 1 large onion, quartered	Position **Disc** in **Bowl** with **slicing side up.** Slice vegetables. When vegetables reach Fill Level, empty into large mixing bowl.
1 pound ground beef, round steak 1½ teaspoons salt ½ teaspoon pepper ¼ cup water	Add meat and seasonings to mixing bowl. Mix well. Press into 2-quart casserole and pour water over top. Roll out pastry on floured surface to shape of casserole.

Cover casserole with pastry. Roll edges to side of casserole and press down with fork. Prick crust several times with fork. Bake until crust is well browned, about 1 hour.

Makes 4 (1-cup) servings

BEEF-ZUCCHINI DINNER 👁 🔵

1 medium onion, ... quartered	Position **Knife Blade** in **Bowl;** add onion. Pulse to chop coarsely.
2 tablespoons butter or margarine **1 pound lean ground beef (page 71)**	In 10-inch skillet melt butter. Add onion; sauté until soft. Add ground beef and brown. Stir occasionally to break up large pieces. Drain fat, if necessary.
1 can (11-oz.) **condensed cream of tomato soup with tomato pieces** **¼ cup water** **1 teaspoon salt** **½ teaspoon pepper**	Stir in soup, water, salt and pepper.
2 medium zucchini **1 large tomato, cut in half**	Position **Disc** in **Bowl** with **slicing side up;** slice zucchini and tomato. Stir slices into meat mixture. Cover and simmer for 30 minutes.

Makes 4 (1-cup) servings

CHEESY MEAT PIE 👁 🔵 🥛

1 unbaked 9-inch pie crust,* chilled (pages 138 & 139) **1 medium onion, quartered**	Preheat oven to 400°F. Position **Knife Blade** in **Bowl;** add onion. Pulse to chop, about 5 seconds.
1 tablespoon butter **½ pound ground beef**	In 10-inch skillet melt butter over medium high heat. Add beef and onion. Brown beef well. Remove from heat; drain off fat.
3 tablespoons all-purpose flour **1 teaspoon salt** **½ teaspoon pepper**	Stir in flour, salt and pepper. Spread beef mixture over pie crust.
8 ounces natural Cheddar cheese, chilled, cut to fit food chute	Position **Disc** in **Bowl** with **shredding side up;** shred cheese. Spread cheese over beef mixture.
1½ cups milk **2 eggs** **1 teaspoon Worcestershire sauce**	Add milk, eggs and Worcestershire sauce to **Blender Jar.** Cover; blend at Stir speed, about 5 seconds.

Pour over meat and cheese. Set pie pan on cookie sheet. Bake until knife inserted in center comes out clean, 30 to 35 minutes. Let cool 10 minutes before serving.

Makes 1 (9-inch) pie

*Mixture fills standard 9-inch pie pan. (See * page 89.)

SAVORY BEEF NOODLES 👁 🔵

2 cups wide noodles	In large saucepan bring 4 cups salted water to a rapid boil. Add noodles. Boil, uncovered, about 5 minutes. (Noodles should be not quite done.) Drain.
1 clove garlic, peeled **1 small onion, quartered** **½ green pepper, cut in 6 pieces (page 38)**	Position **Knife Blade** in **Bowl.** Drop garlic through food chute with Processor running and mince. Turn off and add onion and green pepper. Pulse to chop medium fine. Leave in **Bowl.**
1 tablespoon vegetable oil **1 pound ground beef (page 71)**	In 10-inch skillet heat oil. Add beef and onion mixture; cook, stirring occasionally, until meat is well browned. Drain off fat.
1 can (15-oz.) tomato sauce with bits **½ teaspoon salt** **¼ teaspoon pepper**	Stir in tomato sauce, salt and pepper. Remove from heat.
8 ounces natural Cheddar cheese, chilled, cut to fit food chute	Position **Disc** in **Bowl** with **shredding side up;** shred cheese. Set aside. Preheat oven to 375°F.*
1 container (16-oz.) creamed cottage cheese **1 tablespoon cornstarch**	Position **Knife Blade** in **Bowl.** Add cottage cheese and cornstarch; process until smooth, about 20 to 30 seconds. Add half the shredded cheese; process 2 to 3 seconds.

Place noodles in shallow, 1½-quart or 8-inch square baking pan. Top with cheese mixture, then meat. Sprinkle with remaining shredded cheese. Bake until bubbly, about 30 minutes.* Let stand 10 minutes before serving.

Makes about 6 (1-cup) servings

*Toast-R-Oven® Toaster: preheat 2 minutes at 350°F.; bake 35 minutes.

Savory Beef Noodles

Pork, Lamb & Veal

SWEET AND SOUR PORK 🌶️〰️

1½ pounds boneless pork roast, partially frozen, cut to fit food chute (page 30)	Position **Disc** in **Bowl** with **slicing side up;** slice pork. Place in mixing bowl.
2 tablespoons cornstarch **2 tablespoons soy sauce** **1 teaspoon salt** **⅛ teaspoon pepper**	Add cornstarch, soy sauce, salt and pepper to meat. Toss to mix. Let stand 30 minutes.
2 medium carrots, peeled **1 green pepper, halved** **1 can (8-oz.) water chestnuts** **1 can (8-oz.) pineapple chunks, drained**	Position **Disc** in **Bowl** with **slicing side up.** Slice carrots, green pepper and water chestnuts. Place in large bowl with pineapple chunks.
⅓ cup water **⅓ cup vinegar** **⅓ cup white or brown sugar** **1 tablespoon cornstarch** **1 tablespoon soy sauce**	Position **Knife Blade** in **Bowl;** add ingredients and process to mix sauce, 2 to 3 seconds. Remove **Knife Blade** and leave mixture in **Bowl.**
2 to 3 tablespoons vegetable oil	Heat oil in 12-inch skillet or wok over very high heat. Stir-fry pork until well browned, about 7 to 8 minutes. Drain off fat.
¼ cup water	Add carrot mixture and water; cover and cook 3 minutes. Add sauce. Reduce to medium heat. Cook, stirring constantly, until clear. Serve hot with rice, if desired.

Makes 4 (1-cup) servings

Sweet & Sour Pork

PORK CHOW MEIN

1 pound lean, boneless pork, cut into cubes	Position **Knife Blade** in **Bowl;** add half pork cubes and distribute evenly. Pulse until meat is coarsely chopped, about 4 to 5 seconds. Repeat with remaining pork. Add meat to 12-inch skillet and cook over medium heat until browned.
4 medium stalks celery, each cut crosswise in thirds 1 medium onion, quartered	Position **Disc** in **Bowl** with **slicing side up;** slice celery and onion. Stir-fry with meat until tender, but still crisp, about 5 minutes.
1 can (16-oz.) bean sprouts, drained 1 cup water ¼ cup soy sauce 2 teaspoons instant chicken or beef bouillon granules	Stir in bean sprouts, water, soy sauce and bouillon granules.
2 tablespoons cornstarch ¼ cup water	Combine cornstarch with water and stir to make a smooth paste. Stir into meat mixture. Cook, stirring constantly, until sauce is thickened and clear.
Chow mein noodles	Serve hot over chow mein noodles.

Makes 6 (¾-cup) servings

VARIATIONS:
Chicken Chow Mein: Substitute 1 pound raw, boned and sliced chicken (page 30) for pork. Use 2 tablespoons oil in skillet and stir-fry chicken 5 to 6 minutes. Makes 6 (¾-cup) servings.

Quickie Chow Mein: Substitute 2 cups diced, cooked turkey, chicken or pork. Stir-fry in 2 tablespoons hot oil 2 to 3 minutes. Makes 4 (1-cup) servings.

PORK CREOLE WITH CORN BREAD

1 pound boneless pork roast,* partially frozen and cut to fit food chute (page 30)	Position **Disc** in **Bowl** with **slicing side up;** slice pork.
1 tablespoon vegetable oil	In 12-inch or electric skillet heat oil over medium heat. Sauté pork until well browned. Drain off all but 1 tablespoon fat.
1 medium onion, halved 1 green pepper, halved	Position **Disc** in **Bowl** with **slicing side up.** Slice vegetables. Add to meat and cook 5 minutes, stirring often. Remove from heat.
2 tablespoons all-purpose flour 1 teaspoon salt 1 teaspoon sugar Dash pepper	Preheat oven to 425°F. Stir flour and seasonings into meat mixture.
1 can (28-oz.) whole tomatoes	Add tomatoes to skillet. Break whole tomatoes into smaller pieces with spoon. Pour into 9-inch square baking pan.
½ cup all-purpose flour ½ cup corn meal 1 tablespoon sugar 2 teaspoons baking powder ½ teaspoon salt 1 egg ½ cup milk 2 tablespoons vegetable oil	Position **Knife Blade** in **Bowl;** add remaining ingredients. Process 5 seconds (do not process any longer, it will make corn bread texture coarse). Spoon batter over pork mixture. Bake until corn bread is golden brown, 15 to 20 minutes.

Makes 6 (1-cup) servings

*Leftover cooked pork (2 cups) may be coarsely chopped and substituted for pork roast. Sauté in hot oil with vegetables.

Pork Chow Mein

Spicy Lamb Curry

SPICY LAMB CURRY 😊

| 2 tablespoons vegetable oil | Add oil to 12-inch or electric skillet and brown meat well on all sides. |
| 1½ pounds lean lamb, cut in 1-inch cubes | |

| 2 medium onions, quartered | Position **Disc** in **Bowl** with **slicing side up;** slice onions and apple. Add to meat. |
| 1 apple, peeled, halved, cored | |

1½ cups water	Add remaining ingredients to meat. Break tomatoes up slightly with spoon. Cover; simmer until meat is tender, about 1½ to 2 hours. Stir occasionally. Add more water if necessary. Uncover and simmer until liquid sauce thickens slightly. Serve over rice with chutney and curry condiments, if desired.
1 can (1-lb.) whole tomatoes	
2 teaspoons salt	
1 to 2 teaspoons curry powder	
1 teaspoon sugar	
¼ teaspoon pepper	

Makes 4 (¾-cup) servings

NOTE: Chutney is the most popular condiment and traditionally served with curry dishes. To prepare other condiments use the Food Processor (when necessary) to chop or shred small amounts of the following: grated coconut, chopped hard-cooked eggs, crisp bacon bits, chopped salted peanuts, raisins, currant jelly, chopped red onion, crushed pineapple.

VEAL CUTLETS WITH MUSHROOMS 👁️😊

1½ pounds veal cutlets	Using a meat hammer or the edge of a heavy plate, pound veal between 2 pieces of wax paper to ¼-inch thickness. Cut into 2-inch squares. Combine flour, salt and pepper in large plastic bag. Add veal shake to coat veal evenly.
⅓ cup all-purpose flour	
1 teaspoon salt	
¼ teaspoon pepper	

| 3 tablespoons vegetable oil | In 12-inch skillet heat oil over high heat. Sauté veal until well browned on both sides. Remove from skillet. |

| 2 large onions, cut in eighths | Position **Knife Blade** in **Bowl;** add onions and parsley. Pulse to chop coarsely. Add onion mixture to skillet and sauté. |
| 4 sprigs parsley | |

| 2 medium stalks celery, each cut crosswise in thirds | Position **Disc** in **Bowl** with **slicing side up;** slice celery. Add to onions and sauté until soft. |

1½ cups water	Return veal to skillet. Add water, sherry, bouillon cubes, basil and thyme. Cover; simmer until veal is tender, about 20 minutes.
2 tablespoons sherry	
2 chicken bouillon cubes	
Dash basil and thyme	

| 8 ounces fresh mushrooms, sliced (page 33) | Stir in mushrooms and cook 5 minutes longer. Serve over noodles, if desired. |

Makes 4 (1-cup) servings

CROQUETTES ❧

1 small onion, ... **quartered**	Position **Knife Blade** in **Bowl;** add onion and Pulse to chop finely.
¼ cup butter or . . . . **margarine** **⅓ cup all-purpose flour**	In 1-quart saucepan melt butter and sauté onion until soft. Stir in flour.
1 cup milk	Add milk and cook over medium-high heat, stirring constantly until mixture thickens.
Filling (below) . . . . **½ teaspoon salt**	Remove from heat and stir in filling and salt. Spread mixture in shallow dish or pie pan and chill 2 hours.
3 slices dry bread . . . . **(about 1⅓ cups** **crumbs)**	Position **Knife Blade** in **Bowl** and crumb bread according to directions on page 21. Dump crumbs out onto sheet of wax paper.
1 egg . . . . **2 tablespoons water**	Position **Knife Blade** in **Bowl;** add egg and water. Pulse to mix, 1 or 2 seconds. Leave in **Bowl.** Cut chilled mixture into 8 equal portions. Using spoon, drop and roll each portion in crumbs. Shape into cones or sausages with hands. Coat with egg mixture and roll again in crumbs. Refrigerate at least 2 hours or overnight.
Vegetable oil for . . . . **deep frying**	In large heavy saucepan or electric deep fryer, heat oil to 375°F. Fry croquettes until deep golden brown, about 2 to 3 minutes. Drain on paper towels and serve warm with sauce.

Makes 8 croquettes

Fillings:

Ham: 2 cups ham cubes coarsely chopped in Processor, 2 teaspoons prepared horseradish (omit salt). Serve with Cheddar Cheese Sauce (page 104).

Seafood: 2 cups canned or cooked fish and 2 medium stalks celery, (cut in 1-inch pieces) coarsely chopped separately in Processor, and 1 teaspoon dill weed. Serve with Hollandaise Sauce (page 104).

Chicken or Turkey: 1½ cups cooked chicken or turkey cubes, 1 can (8-oz.) water chestnuts drained, finely chopped in Processor, and ⅛ teaspoon ginger. Serve with Fresh Mushroom Sauce (page 103).

Ham Croquettes with Cheddar Cheese Sauce (page 104)

Processor Pizza

PROCESSOR PIZZA

1 recipe Basic White Bread dough (page 122)	Prepare dough and let rise until doubled in size, about 1½ hours. Punch down; turn out onto floured board; cover; let rest for 15 minutes.
10 sprigs parsley	Position **Knife Blade** in **Bowl.** Add parsley. Pulse to chop. Set aside.
8 ounces natural Swiss cheese, chilled	Position **Disc** in **Bowl** with **shredding side up;** shred cheese. Set aside.
2 ounces fresh Parmesan cheese	Grate cheese as directed on page 14. Add to Swiss cheese and stir to mix.
1 large onion, quartered 1 clove garlic, peeled	Position **Knife Blade** in **Bowl.** Add onion and garlic; process to chop finely.
2 tablespoons vegetable oil	In 10-inch skillet heat oil; sauté onion and garlic.
1 can (16-oz.) tomato sauce 1 can (6-oz.) tomato paste 2 teaspoons sugar 1 teaspoon basil 1 teaspoon oregano ½ teaspoon salt	Stir in tomato sauce and paste, sugar, herbs and salt. Simmer, uncovered, for 15 minutes.
Pepperoni slices (page 42), ripe olives or mushroom slices	Preheat oven to 450°F. On floured surface, roll out half the bread dough to form a 13-inch circle.

Fit into greased pizza pan or cookie sheet. Brush lightly with olive or vegetable oil. Spread with half the tomato mixture. Sprinkle with half the cheese mixture, then half the parsley. Top with pepperoni slices. Repeat with remaining dough. Bake 15 to 20 minutes. Serve hot.

Makes 2 (13-inch) pizzas

SKILLET HASH

Use up leftovers this great, traditional way.

1 medium onion, quartered 2 to 3 medium potatoes, diced, cooked	Position **Knife Blade** in **Bowl.** Separately process onion and potatoes. Pulse to chop coarsely. (Do not overprocess potatoes; they get rubbery.) Transfer to large mixing bowl.
2 cups cooked beef or corned beef, cut in 1-inch cubes	Position **Knife Blade** in **Bowl.** Add beef cubes; Pulse to chop coarsely. Add to mixing bowl.
2 eggs 2 tablespoons catsup ½ to 1 teaspoon salt ⅛ teaspoon pepper	Add remaining ingredients to meat mixture and stir well.
3 tablespoons vegetable oil	In 12-inch skillet, heat oil over medium heat. Spread meat mixture in skillet. Fry each side until brown, about 5 minutes; turn with a spatula. Hash will be moist and crumbly.

Makes 4 (1¼-cup) servings

FETTUCCINI ALFREDO

4 ounces fresh Parmesan cheese	Grate cheese as directed on page 14. Set aside.
1 package (12-oz.) fettuccini or egg noodles	Cook noodles as directed on package. Drain well. Transfer to large dish.
1 cup whipping cream ¼ cup soft butter or margarine, cut in 4 pieces Dash pepper	Position **Knife Blade** in **Bowl;** add remaining ingredients. Pulse until thick and creamy, about 10 seconds. Do not overbeat.

Add to hot noodles and toss until evenly covered. Serve.

Makes 8 (1-cup) servings

NOTE: Recipe may be halved.

Baked Fish with Piquant Stuffing, Chicken Cacciatore

Poultry, fish and seafood have always played a role in American cooking. They're suitable for both everyday and festive occasions. Let the Food Processor introduce you to new ways of serving these foods, as well as some Food Processor methods of preparing traditional favorites.

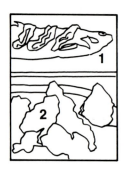

1. Baked Fish with Piquant Stuffing (page 83)
2. Chicken Cacciatore (below)

CHICKEN-TIME TANGO

4 medium onions, halved 4 medium green peppers, halved	Position **Disc** in **Bowl** with **slicing side up.** Slice onions and peppers.
2 tablespoons butter or margarine	In 10-inch skillet melt butter. Sauté onions and peppers until soft.
1 can (10½-oz.) condensed cream of chicken soup ¾ cup Chablis or other dry white wine ½ teaspoon thyme leaves Salt and pepper to taste	Add soup, wine and seasonings to onions and peppers; stir and continue heating until mixture is smooth.
1 can (8-oz.) water chestnuts, drained	Position **Disc** in **Bowl** with **slicing side up;** slice water chestnuts.
5 cups diced, cooked chicken	Stir chicken and water chestnuts into sauce mixture. Cover and simmer for 15 minutes. Add additional chicken broth or water if necessary. Serve over rice.

Makes 6 (1-cup) servings

CHICKEN CACCIATORE

2- to 2½-pound frying chicken, cut in 8 pieces ¼ cup vegetable oil	In 12-inch or electric skillet heat oil over medium high heat. Add chicken and brown on all sides. Drain off fat if necessary.
4 sprigs parsley 1 clove garlic, peeled 1 medium onion, quartered	Position **Knife Blade** in **Bowl.** Add parsley. Drop garlic through food chute with Processor running and mince. Turn off. Add onion; Pulse to chop medium fine.
1 can (16-oz.) whole tomatoes 1 teaspoon salt ½ teaspoon oregano ¼ teaspoon basil ⅛ teaspoon pepper	Add tomatoes and seasonings. Pulse 1 or 2 times to break up tomatoes. Pour over chicken. Cover and simmer until chicken is tender, 30 to 40 minutes.

Makes 4 servings (2 pieces each)

NOTE: If thicker sauce is desired, remove chicken to serving dish. Combine 1 tablespoon flour and 1 tablespoon water to make a smooth paste. Stir into sauce. Cook, stirring constantly, until slightly thickened.

Crunchy Chicken Casserole

Creamy Chicken Crepes with Velouté Sauce (page 103)

CRUNCHY CHICKEN CASSEROLE 🌙💲

2 large carrots, peeled	. . .Position **Disc** in **Bowl** with **slicing side up;** slice carrots. Bring 1 cup salted water to a boil; add carrots. Cover; simmer until not quite tender, about 15 minutes. Drain.
8 ounces natural Cheddar cheese, chilled **¼ cup butter** **¼ cup all-purpose flour** **1 can (10¾-oz.) chicken broth** **4 cups diced, cooked chicken** **1 jar (2-oz.) chopped pimiento**	. . . . . .Position **Disc** in **Bowl** with **shredding side up.** Shred cheese; leave in **Bowl.** In 3-quart saucepan melt butter over medium heat. Stir in flour. Then, add broth, stirring constantly, until mixture thickens. Lower heat and add cheese. Stir until cheese melts. Remove from heat. Stir in chicken, carrots and pimiento. Spread in shallow, 2-quart casserole. Preheat oven to 375°F.
¼ cup butter **8 ounces herb seasoned stuffing**	. . . . .In 10-inch skillet melt butter. Add stuffing and mix with butter. Spread over chicken mixture. Bake for 30 minutes.

Makes 8 (1-cup) servings

CREAMY CHICKEN CREPES 🐚

1 recipe Basic Blender Crepes (page 129)	. . .Prepare crepes. Set aside.
2 packages (10-oz. each) frozen broccoli	. . . . . .Cook broccoli until not quite done; drain. Separate into spears, cut each spear in half lengthwise; set aside.
1 small onion, quartered	. . . . .Position **Knife Blade** in **Bowl.** Add onion. Pulse to chop finely. Transfer to large mixing bowl.
3 cups diced, cooked chicken **1 can (10¾-oz.) condensed cream of mushroom soup** **1 recipe Velouté Sauce (page 103)**	. . . . .Preheat oven to 450°F. Position **Knife Blade** in **Bowl.** Add half the chicken. Pulse to chop coarsely. Add to onion and repeat with remaining chicken. Mix mushroom soup into onion/chicken mixture. Spread 2 slightly rounded tablespoonfuls mixture down center of each crepe.

Position 2 broccoli spears on top of chicken mixture with flowerets at either edge. Roll up crepe. In shallow, 2-quart baking dish, place filled crepes, close together, layering as needed. Prepare sauce and pour over filled crepes. Bake 10 to 15 minutes.

Makes 12 filled crepes
(6 servings)

NOTE: Crepes and filling may be made the day before and refrigerated. Fill and bake just before serving.

CORN BREAD DRESSING

1 package (8-oz.) corn bread stuffing	Preheat oven to 375°F. Empty stuffing into large mixing bowl.
4 tablespoons butter **¾ cup boiling water**	Melt butter in water. Pour over stuffing and toss.
1 package (10-oz.) precooked sausage lengths, partially frozen, sliced (page 30) **2 tablespoons butter**	Position **Disc** in **Bowl** with **slicing side up.** Slice sausage. In 10-inch skillet brown meat over medium-high heat. Add to stuffing mixture, leaving drippings in skillet. Add butter to drippings and melt.
4 medium stalks celery, each cut in 1-inch pieces **1 medium onion, quartered**	Position **Knife Blade** in **Bowl.** Add celery and Pulse to chop coarsely, about 3 to 4 seconds. Add to skillet. Repeat with onion.
½ teaspoon poultry seasoning	Sauté celery and onion until tender. Add celery mixture and poultry seasoning to stuffing.
1 egg **¼ cup water**	Position **Knife Blade** in **Bowl;** add egg and water; process 3 to 4 seconds.

Toss with stuffing mixture. (If mixture is dry, add about 2 tablespoons more water.) Use to stuff bird* or place in a greased, 2-quart casserole. Cover and bake 35 to 40 minutes. For a more crisp dressing, uncover and cook 5 minutes longer.

Makes 5 cups stuffing
(Enough for an 8- to 10-pound bird)

*Bake any stuffing that does not fit in bird in casserole after bird has been roasted.

TRADITIONAL BREAD STUFFING

1 loaf (1-lb.) day old bread, (20 slices) (page 14)	Crumb bread. As bread reaches Fill Level, empty bread crumbs into large container. (Bread may be crumbed the day before and left uncovered to dry.)
5 sprigs parsley	Position **Knife Blade** in **Bowl;** add parsley. Pulse until coarsely chopped. Add to bread.
4 medium stalks celery, each cut crosswise in thirds **4 to 8 ounces fresh mushrooms** **1 large onion, quartered**	Position **Disc** in **Bowl** with **slicing side up** and slice vegetables.
¾ cup butter or margarine	In 12-inch skillet melt butter. Sauté vegetables until soft.
1 chicken bouillon cube, dissolved in ¾ cup hot water **2 teaspoons poultry seasoning** **2 teaspoons salt** **¼ teaspoon pepper**	Add dissolved bouillon liquid and seasonings to vegetables. Stir to mix.
Cooked giblets (optional)	Position **Knife Blade** in **Bowl;** add giblets. Pulse until coarsely chopped.

Add giblets and vegetable mixture to bread; toss to combine. Stuff bird with mixture just before roasting and roast in usual manner. (Any extra stuffing can be placed in a greased casserole. Cover, if desired, and bake at 375°F. for 40 to 45 minutes, after the bird has been roasted.)

Makes 5 to 6 cups stuffing
(Enough for a 12- to 14-pound bird)

Corn Bread Dressing

VEGETABLE FISH BAKE

3 medium onions, cut to fit food chute **2 tablespoons butter**	Preheat oven to 350°F. Position **Disc** in **Bowl** with **slicing side up**; slice onions. Arrange on bottom of greased 9-inch square baking dish. Dot with butter.
1 pound frozen fillets of sole, thawed, drained **Salt and pepper**	Season both sides of sole with salt and pepper. Arrange on top of onions.
4 large mushrooms **1 green pepper, halved** **2 whole pimientos**	Position **Disc** in **Bowl** with **slicing side up**; slice mushrooms, pepper and pimiento. Spread evenly over fish.
¼ cup dry white wine **1 tablespoon lemon juice**	Combine wine and lemon juice. Pour over vegetables.

Bake until sole flakes easily when tested with a fork, 25 to 30 minutes.

Makes 4 (1-cup) servings

BAKED FISH WITH PIQUANT STUFFING

2- to 2½-pound whole fish, cleaned, dressed **Salt**	Pat fish dry. Sprinkle salt over inside of fish. Preheat oven to 375°F.
½ cup butter or margarine **1 small onion, quartered** **1 medium stalk celery, cut in 1-inch pieces** **5 sprigs parsley** **½ teaspoon salt** **¼ teaspoon poultry seasoning** **Dash garlic powder**	In 12-inch or electric skillet melt butter over low heat. Position **Knife Blade** in **Bowl**. Add onion, celery and parsley. Pulse to chop medium fine, 5 to 6 seconds. Add chopped vegetables and seasonings to skillet. Increase heat to medium-high and sauté, stirring occasionally, for 2 minutes.
4 slices fresh bread, each broken in 4 pieces	Position **Knife Blade** in **Bowl**. Add bread; Pulse to chop medium fine, 7 to 10 seconds. Add to skillet, stir to mix thoroughly. Remove from heat.
2 slices bacon, cut in half crosswise **Paprika** **Lemon slices** **Parsley**	Lightly grease slotted cover portion of broil pan. Place fish on top of broil pan; stuff with bread mixture. Top with bacon and sprinkle with paprika.

Bake until fish flakes easily with fork, about 30 minutes. Place under broiler to crisp bacon, if desired. Garnish with lemon slices and parsley.

Makes 4 (2-inch) servings

Sunday Codfish Cakes

SUNDAY CODFISH CAKES

Serve Codfish Cakes with baked beans for a traditional Downeast meal.

1 small onion, quartered **8 sprigs parsley**	Position **Knife Blade** in **Bowl**. Add onion and parsley. Pulse to chop coarsely, 2 to 3 seconds.
2 cups boiled potatoes (about 2 medium), cut in 1-inch pieces **2 eggs** **3 tablespoons butter, melted** **½ teaspoon salt** **⅛ teaspoon pepper**	Add potatoes, eggs, butter and seasonings to **Bowl**; Pulse to mix, 5 to 7 seconds.
1 pound cooked, drained codfish*, cut in 2-inch pieces	Add codfish; Pulse to mix, 2 to 3 seconds. Mixture should be slightly coarse. Chill mixture in refrigerator for at least 1 hour. Shape into round, flat cakes using ⅓ cup amounts (about 3-inch diameter).
½ to ¾ cup seasoned bread crumbs	Coat with seasoned bread crumbs.
⅓ cup vegetable oil	In 12-inch skillet heat oil over medium high heat; add cakes; cook until golden brown, 4 to 5 minutes per side. Repeat with remaining cakes.

Makes 9 to 10 (3-inch) cakes

*NOTE: Codfish may be baked or poached just until it flakes easily when tested with a fork.

QUENELLES 〜

These delicate fish dumplings originated in France.

1 tablespoon butter . . . . . Position **Knife Blade** in **Bowl;** add butter; Pulse until butter is broken up.

1 pound bay scallops, fresh or frozen and thawed . . . . Add scallops to **Bowl;** process for 1 minute; stop twice and scrape down sides of **Bowl.**

1 egg
½ teaspoon salt
¼ teaspoon nutmeg
⅛ teaspoon pepper
4 drops hot pepper sauce
1½ cups heavy cream . . . . Add egg and seasonings; Pulse to mix, 3 to 4 seconds. Scrape down sides of **Bowl.** Pour heavy cream in a steady stream through food chute with Processor running. Process until mixture is smooth, about 1 minute. Stop twice to scrape down sides of **Bowl.** Remove **Knife Blade** and chill mixture for at least 30 minutes. The colder the mixture is, without freezing, the easier it will be to shape.

1 tablespoon butter . . . . . Heavily butter a cold large electric skillet. Select 2 equal-size serving spoons, about 3 inches long. See directions below for shaping quenelles.

2 quarts water . . . . Meanwhile, bring water to a boil. Gently pour along side of skillet. Turn temperature control to about 200°F; simmer gently, uncovered, for 5 minutes. (Simmer time starts when small bubbles can be seen in water.) Carefully turn quenelles and simmer 5 minutes longer. Using slotted spoon, remove quenelles and drain on paper towel for a few seconds.

1 recipe Fresh Mushroom Sauce (page 103) . . . . Transfer to a warm platter and spoon sauce over. Serve immediately.

Makes 15 to 16 quenelles (about 6 servings)

To shape quenelles: Use spoons to shape quenelles by first dipping them into a bowl filled with boiling or very hot water. Then, use one spoon to place a single heaping amount of mixture onto the other spoon. Dip the empty spoon into the hot water again and use it to smooth the top and sides of the quenelle on the other spoon. Scrape around the sides to remove the excess mixture. Gently place each shaped quenelle into the cold buttered skillet, carefully placing them close together, but not touching. Repeat this procedure until all the mixture is used.

HOW TO SHAPE AND POACH QUENELLES

Dip 2 serving spoons into hot water; use them to shape quenelles as described in recipe above.

Space quenelles carefully in skillet; very close, but not touching.

Pour boiling water carefully along side of skillet. Never pour water directly onto quenelles.

TANGY TUNA TETRAZZINI

½ of 1-lb. package linguine 1 teaspoon salt	Add linguine and salt to 3 quarts of rapidly boiling water; boil for 8 to 10 minutes, cooking until slightly underdone. Drain.
4 ounces Parmesan cheese	Position **Knife Blade** in **Bowl** with **Disc** above it, **shredding side up;** process until cheese reaches desired fineness.
1 can (7-oz.) tuna, drained 1 can (10¾-oz.) condensed cream of celery soup	Preheat oven to 375°F. Position **Knife Blade** in **Bowl;** add tuna and soup. Process to mix, about 2 to 3 seconds.
1 package (10-oz.) chopped broccoli, cooked, drained ½ cup almond slivers	Place half of linguine in shallow 1½-quart or 8-inch square baking dish. Cover with chopped broccoli and half the Parmesan cheese. Add remaining linguine; pour tuna mixture over linguine. Sprinkle with second half of cheese and then almond slivers. Bake for 30 minutes.

Makes 6 (1-cup) servings

TUNA SUPPER

3 slices fresh bread, folded	Position **Disc** in **Bowl** with **shredding side up.** Shred bread.
2 tablespoons butter or margarine	In 10-inch skillet melt butter over medium heat. Add bread crumbs and sauté until golden brown. Transfer to small mixing bowl.
8 ounces natural Cheddar cheese, chilled, cut to fit food chute	Position **Disc** in **Bowl** with **shredding side up.** Shred cheese.
2 tablespoons butter 2 tablespoons all-purpose flour 1 can (10¾-oz.) condensed chicken broth, undiluted	In same skillet melt butter over medium heat. Mix in flour to make a smooth paste. Add chicken broth; cook, stirring constantly, until thickened and smooth.
2 cans (6½-oz. each) tuna, drained, flaked 1 can (16-oz.) Chinese vegetables, drained	Stir in tuna, vegetables and shredded cheese. Simmer over low heat until cheese melts and mixture is thoroughly heated, about 10 minutes.

Sprinkle with sautéed bread crumbs and serve.

Makes 4 (1-cup) servings

Quenelles with Fresh Mushroom Sauce (page 103)

Shrimp Jambalaya

CRAB CASSOULETTES ✎

1 slice fresh bread, **quartered**	Position **Knife Blade** in **Bowl;** add bread. Pulse to chop bread finely, 7 to 10 seconds.
1 tablespoon butter **or margarine**	In 10-inch skillet melt butter over medium heat. Brown bread crumbs. Set aside on paper towels.
1 small onion, **quartered** **1 large stalk celery,** **cut in 1-inch** **pieces** **¼ green pepper, cut** **in 3 pieces**	Position **Knife Blade** in **Bowl;** add vegetables. Pulse to chop finely, 4 to 5 seconds.
¼ cup butter or **margarine**	Preheat oven to 375°F. In skillet melt butter; stir in vegetables. Sauté over medium heat until soft.
3 tablespoons **all-purpose flour** **1½ cups half and half** **1 teaspoon dry** **mustard** **½ teaspoon** **Worcestershire** **sauce** **¼ teaspoon salt** **Dash pepper and** **hot pepper sauce**	Stir in flour; reduce heat to simmer temperature. Add half and half and seasonings. Cook, stirring constantly, until thickened.
2 cups cooked rice **5 to 6 ounces** **(1½-cups) frozen** **or canned** **crabmeat, drained,** **flaked, picked over** **for tendons** **1 jar (2-oz.) pimiento,** **drained**	Stir in rice, crabmeat and pimiento. Divide mixture equally into 4 1½-cup baking dishes. Sprinkle bread crumbs over tops. Bake until golden brown and bubbly, about 15 minutes.

Makes about 4 (1-cup) servings

SHRIMP JAMBALAYA ✎ ✇

A Creole dish made with a variety of meats, but always with rice and tomatoes.

3 tablespoons butter **or margarine**	In 3-quart heavy saucepan melt butter over low heat.
1 small clove garlic, **peeled** **1 medium green** **pepper, cut in** **12 pieces**	Position **Knife Blade** in **Bowl.** Drop garlic through food chute with Processor running. Add green pepper; Pulse to chop medium coarse, 4 to 5 seconds. Add to saucepan and sauté.
1 small onion, **quartered** **4 to 6 precooked pork** **sausages*, partially** **frozen**	Position **Disc** in **Bowl** with **slicing side up;** slice onion and sausage. Add to saucepan and sauté 5 minutes.
1 can (16-oz.) whole **tomatoes**	Add tomatoes to saucepan and break tomatoes into pieces with spoon.
2 to 3 cups **(about 1 pound)** **raw, cleaned shrimp** **2 cups water** **1 bay leaf** **1 teaspoon salt** **⅛ teaspoon pepper** **Dash cayenne** **pepper**	Thaw shrimp, if frozen, and add shrimp, water and seasonings to saucepan; bring to boil.
1 cup uncooked rice	Stir in rice; reduce heat to simmer. Cover and cook until rice is fluffy, about 30 minutes. Remove bay leaf.

Makes 6 (1-cup) servings

*One cup chopped ham may be substituted for pork sausage.

VARIATION:
Chicken Jambalaya: Substitute 2 to 3 cups cooked chicken or turkey meat for shrimp.

SEASHORE STUFFED CLAMS

A New England favorite, especially when made with Quahog clams.

1 dozen large	Prepare as directed below.
hard-shell clams	

¼ cup butter or	In 10-inch skillet melt butter over low heat. Position **Knife Blade** in **Bowl.** Drop garlic through food chute with Processor running and mince. Turn off. Add onion and celery. Pulse to chop finely. Add to butter. Increase heat and sauté, stirring frequently.
margarine	
1 small clove garlic, peeled	
1 medium onion, quartered	
1 large stalk celery, cut in 1-inch pieces	

4 slices fresh	Position **Knife Blade** in **Bowl.** Add bread. Process until crumbed, about 30 seconds. Add to skillet, then stir in seasonings.
sandwich bread, any flavor, each quartered	
½ teaspoon poultry seasoning	
½ teaspoon salt	

Preheat oven to 400°F. Position **Knife Blade** in **Bowl.** Add clams. Pulse to chop, about 4 to 5 Pulses. Add to skillet. Cook until clam juice is absorbed. Fill 12 well-greased clam shells with a heaping tablespoonful of clam mixture. Sprinkle tops with paprika, if desired. Bake until golden brown and hot, about 10 to 15 minutes.

Makes 12 clam halves
(about 4 servings)

To prepare clams: Soak clams in bowl of cold salted water for about 30 minutes. To remove grit and sand, wash shells well. To ease opening clams, spread in large baking pan. Place under broiler, watching carefully, until clam shells open just a fraction, about 5 minutes. Remove from oven and allow clams to cool slightly. Insert knife between shell halves; carefully cut around to shell hinge, forcing shells apart. Loosen clam meat (all of it is edible) from shell and place in strainer or sieve. Reserve 12 clam shells; set them aside in baking dish. Rinse clam meat thoroughly under cold running water. Spread on paper towels to drain. Pat dry.

NOTE: Baked clams can be frozen; reheat right from the freezer at 400°F. until hot and bubbly.

Seashore Stuffed Clams

Country-Fare
Eggs & Cheese

Eggs and cheese, separately or as partners, can be served at any meal of the day. Don't hesitate to make gourmet specialties, like Quiche Lorraine or Swiss Fondue. They began as simple, thrifty peasant meals, and today are classic favorites.

QUICHE LORRAINE 🥧👁

A tasty bacon and cheese pie from the Lorraine district of France.

1 unbaked 9-inch pie crust,* chilled (pages 138 & 139)	Preheat oven to 400°F.
8 ounces natural Swiss cheese, chilled	Position **Disc** in **Bowl** with **shredding side up;** shred cheese. Transfer to mixing bowl.
8 slices cooked bacon, broken in pieces **4 eggs**	Position **Knife Blade** in **Bowl;** add bacon and eggs. Process until bacon is chopped, about 10 seconds. Pour over cheese.
1¾ cups milk **1 teaspoon chives** **½ teaspoon salt** **¼ teaspoon pepper**	Add milk, chives, salt and pepper to cheese mixture. Stir to mix thoroughly. Pour into crust.
Nutmeg	Sprinkle surface with nutmeg.

Bake until knife inserted in center comes out clean, 30 to 35 minutes. Let cool 10 minutes before serving.

Makes 1 (9-inch) pie

*Mixture fills a standard 9-inch pie pan. If using shallow, ready-made 9-inch pie shells, bake remaining filling in custard cups at same temperature.

VARIATION:
Bacon Spinach Pie: Decrease cheese to 4 ounces. Clean and dry 2 cups fresh spinach; add to **Bowl.** With **Knife Blade,** Pulse to chop coarsely, 2 to 3 times. Stir into custard mixture.

EGG FOO YONG 👁🥚

4 ounces fresh mushrooms	Position **Knife Blade** in **Bowl** with **Disc** above it, **slicing side up.** Coarsely chop mushrooms (page 32.)
1 medium stalk celery, cut in 1-inch pieces **1 small onion, quartered**	Position **Knife Blade** in **Bowl.** Add celery and onion to **Bowl.** Pulse to chop coarsely. Empty into mixing bowl.
¼ green pepper, cut in 3 pieces **½ cup cooked meat, seafood or poultry, cut in 1-inch pieces**	Position **Knife Blade** in **Bowl.** Coarsely chop green pepper and meat separately. Combine with onion and celery in mixing bowl.
1 egg **1 teaspoon soy sauce** **Pinch ginger (optional)**	Position **Knife Blade** in **Bowl;** add egg, soy sauce and ginger. Pulse 2 or 3 times. Mix with ingredients in bowl.
3 tablespoons vegetable oil	At serving time, heat oil in 10-inch skillet over high heat. Using ⅓-cup measure, shape mixture into patties. With metal spatula, place patties in skillet. Cook about 3 minutes. Turn and cook other side.

Sauce:

1 teaspoon cornstarch **¼ cup water** **2 teaspoons soy sauce**	In 1-quart saucepan combine cornstarch with water and soy sauce, mixing until smooth. Cook, stirring constantly, over medium high heat, until clear. Serve hot over patties.

Makes 6 (2½-inch) patties

SCRAMBLED EGGS 🫗

3 eggs **3 tablespoons milk or cream** **¼ teaspoon salt** **Dash pepper**	Place eggs, milk, salt and pepper in **Blender Jar.** Cover. Blend at Stir speed, 2 to 3 seconds.
1 tablespoon butter or margarine	In 8-inch skillet melt butter over low heat.

Add egg mixture. Stir from outside edge toward center, allowing uncooked egg to flow to outside. Continue stirring until all egg is cooked and has creamy appearance.

Makes 2 (½-cup) servings

FAVORITE CHEESE SOUFFLE

8 ounces natural Cheddar cheese, chilled, cut to fit food chute	Preheat oven to 350°F. Position **Disc** in **Bowl** with **shredding side up.** Shred cheese; leave in **Bowl.**
¼ cup butter **¼ cup all-purpose flour** **2 teaspoons dry mustard** **1 cup milk**	In 2-quart saucepan melt butter; stir in flour and mustard. Remove from heat and add milk. Cook over medium heat, stirring constantly, until thickened. Add cheese and continue stirring until cheese melts and mixture is smooth. Remove from heat.
5 egg yolks, slightly beaten	Add egg yolks to cheese sauce and mix well. Cook 2 more minutes. Remove from heat and set aside.
5 egg whites **¼ teaspoon cream of tartar**	In large bowl, combine egg whites and cream of tartar.

Beat until stiff, but not dry. (Egg whites are stiff enough when bowl can be inverted and whites will not fall out.) Gently fold cheese sauce into egg whites by hand. Pour into greased 2-quart souffle dish or straight-sided casserole. Bake until set, about 50 minutes.

Makes 1 (2-quart) souffle

FRENCH OMELET

1 tablespoon butter or margarine	In 7-inch skillet melt butter over low heat.
2 eggs **¼ cup milk** **⅛ teaspoon salt**	Position **Knife Blade** in **Bowl.** Add eggs, milk and salt. Process to mix, 2 to 3 seconds.

Pour into skillet. Cook slowly, lifting edges so uncooked egg flows underneath. When almost firm, loosen edges and lift one side to fold in half as you tip skillet. Slide off skillet onto hot serving plate.

Makes 1 serving

NOTE: Omelet may be filled with any of the following: 1 ounce natural Cheddar or Swiss cheese, shredded; ½ cup fresh sliced mushrooms, sautéed in 1 tablespoon butter; ¼ cup chopped ham; 2 slices crisp crumbled bacon.

VARIATION:
Spanish Omelet: Position **Knife Blade** in **Bowl** and add 1 small tomato, quartered, 1 small onion, quartered, and ¼ green pepper, cut in 3 pieces. Pulse to chop coarsely. Spoon half into omelet just before folding. Spoon remainder over top.

HOW TO MAKE A SOUFFLE

Position Disc in Bowl, shredding side up. Shred cheese. Add egg yolks to smooth cheese mixture.

Beat egg whites and cream of tartar with mixer. Whites should be stiff, but not dry, (see recipe above).

Fold cheese mixture into egg whites gently, using rubber spatula. Pour into souffle dish carefully.

SWISS CHEESE FONDUE ☍ ◉

1 pound natural Swiss cheese, chilled, cut to fit food chute	. . .Position **Knife Blade** in **Bowl** with **Disc** above it, **shredding side up;** shred cheese. As shredded cheese reaches Fill Level, empty into mixing bowl.
2 teaspoons cornstarch ¼ teaspoon salt Dash pepper Dash nutmeg	. . . . .Add cornstarch, salt, pepper and nutmeg to cheese. Toss lightly with a fork to combine.
1 cup dry white wine	. . . . .Add wine to 3-quart saucepan and cook over low heat until it begins to bubble gently. Add cheese, a handful at a time, stirring vigorously with wooden spoon until cheese melts and mixture is thoroughly blended.
1 loaf crusty French bread, cut in 1-inch cubes	. . . . .Serve immediately with bread cubes.

Makes 2 cups

SHARP CHEESY RAREBIT ◉

Serve this delicious and easy dish for luncheon.

12 slices bacon	. . . . .Cook bacon; drain on paper towels.
4 slices fresh sandwich bread, any kind	. . . . .Toast bread. Quarter each slice and arrange in 4 soup dishes.
1 pound natural sharp Cheddar cheese, chilled ¼ cup all-purpose flour 2 to 3 teaspoons dry mustard ½ teaspoon salt	. . . . . .Position **Disc** in **Bowl** with **shredding side up.** Shred cheese. As shredded cheese reaches Fill Level, empty into large plastic bag. Add flour, mustard and salt to cheese; twist bag closed and shake to mix.
1½ cups milk 1 teaspoon Worcestershire sauce	. . . . .Add milk to 3-quart saucepan. Place over medium low heat. When milk begins to simmer, gradually add cheese by handfuls, stirring constantly.

Continue heating until sauce is smooth and cheese has melted. Rarebit will be thick at first but thins out as cheese melts. Stir in Worcestershire sauce. Pour rarebit over toast; top with bacon slices. Serve immediately.

Makes 4 (¾-cup) servings

Favorite Cheese Souffle

Fresh & Tangy
Salads & Dressings

The Food Processor shines when it comes to salads. It helps you make old favorites and acquaints you with new combinations. Chopping, shredding and slicing are a secret of salad variety, and that's what the Processor does.

Invent your own salads: almost any fruit or vegetable can make a salad. Add meat, fish, eggs or cheese and you have a main dish. Discover the pride and pleasure of serving your own freshly made mayonnaise, as well as the many different dressings you can make from just a few basic recipes.

1. Special Vinaigrette Dressing, page 101
2. French Dressing, page 101
3. Oil and Vinegar Dressing, page 101

PROCESSOR CHEF SALAD

1 small onion, ... quartered 2 hard-cooked eggs, cut in half	Position **Knife Blade** in **Bowl.** Add onion and eggs to **Bowl.** Pulse until coarsely chopped. Transfer to salad bowl.
¼ pound Swiss . . . . cheese, chilled	Position **Disc** in **Bowl** with **shredding side up.** Shred cheese. Add to salad bowl.
¼ pound sliced boiled . . . ham ½ medium head iceberg lettuce, cut in 1-inch wedges	Position **Disc** in **Bowl** with **slicing side up.** Cross-cut ham (page 31), then slice lettuce. When lettuce reaches Fill Level, empty lettuce and ham into salad bowl. Slice remaining lettuce; add to salad bowl.
Salt and pepper . . . . Dill weed Salad dressing	Season with salt, pepper, and dill weed. Add salad dressing of your choice. Toss well.

Makes 2 (2-cup) servings

HAWAIIAN CHICKEN SALAD

½ cup walnuts	Position **Disc** in **Bowl** with **slicing side up;** slice walnuts. Transfer to a large mixing bowl.
3 large stalks celery, ... each cut crosswise in thirds ¼ head iceberg lettuce, cut in 1-inch wedges	Position **Disc** in **Bowl** with **slicing side up.** Slice celery; add to nuts. Repeat with lettuce and add to nuts.
3 cups cooked, boned, . . . cubed chicken	Position **Knife Blade** in **Bowl.** Add 1½ cups chicken. Pulse to chop coarsely 3 or 4 times. Add to nut mixture and repeat with remaining chicken.
1 can (20-oz.) . . . . pineapple chunks, drained ¾ cup mayonnaise ½ to 1 teaspoon salt ¼ teaspoon pepper	Add pineapple, mayonnaise, salt and pepper. Toss well. Serve on lettuce leaves, if desired.

Makes 8 (¾-cup) servings

HOT POTATO SALAD

4 slices bacon	Preheat oven to 400°F. Fry bacon in 10-inch skillet until crisp. Set bacon aside; leave bacon fat in skillet.
1 small onion, ... quartered 6 sprigs parsley	Position **Knife Blade** in **Bowl;** add onion and parsley. Pulse until evenly chopped. Add to skillet and sauté until onion is soft. Remove from heat.
⅓ cup vinegar . . . . ¼ cup water ½ teaspoon salt ¼ teaspoon pepper	Crumble bacon and add to skillet, along with vinegar, water, salt and pepper. Stir to mix.
6 medium potatoes, ... peeled, halved	Position **Disc** in **Bowl** with **slicing side up;** slice potatoes. Empty **Bowl** into skillet as potatoes reach Fill Level.

Mix potatoes with vinegar mixture and transfer to a shallow, 2-quart casserole. Cover and bake 1 hour or until potatoes are done. Serve hot or cold.

Makes 10 (½-cup) servings

Processor Chef Salad

CHICKEN 'N ORANGE SALAD 🌀

2 chicken breasts, ... Position **Disc** in **Bowl** with
  split, cooked, **slicing side up.** Slice
  boned chicken (be sure it is well
2 medium stalks boned), celery, pepper
  celery, each cut and onion. Transfer to large
  crosswise in thirds serving bowl.
1 medium green
  pepper, halved
1 medium onion,
  halved

2 cans (11-oz. each) .... Add mandarin orange seg-
  mandarin orange ments and mayonnaise to
  segments, drained chicken mixture. Toss well
½ cup mayonnaise and serve over crisp lettuce
  (page 100) leaves.

Makes 6 (1-cup) servings

SALMON SHOESTRING SALAD 🌀 🌀

A surprisingly refreshing, easy main dish salad.

4 large carrots, peeled, .. Position **Disc** in **Bowl** with
  cut to fit food chute **shredding side up;** shred
  (page 12) carrots. Transfer to large
  mixing bowl.

¼ head iceberg lettuce, ... Position **Disc** in **Bowl** with
  cut in 1-inch wedges **slicing side up;** slice let-
1 small onion, tuce and onion. Add to
  quartered carrots.

1 can (1-lb.) salmon, ... Add salmon, mayonnaise
  drained, boned, and mustard to carrots; stir
  flaked to mix thoroughly.
1 cup mayonnaise
  (page 100)
½ teaspoon prepared
  mustard

2 cans (1½-oz. each) ..... Just before serving, add
  shoestring potatoes potatoes and toss.

(Potatoes will get soggy if added to salad too soon.)

Makes 8 (¾-cup) servings

CREAMY CUCUMBER SALAD 🌀

2 small cucumbers ..... Position **Disc** in **Bowl** with
2 medium red onions, **slicing side up.** Slice cu-
  halved cumbers and onions. As
  sliced vegetables reach
  Fill Level, empty into large
  serving bowl.

½ cup mayonnaise ...... Add remaining ingredients.
1 tablespoon dried Toss well.
  parsley flakes
1 teaspoon lemon juice
½ teaspoon sugar

Makes 8 (¾-cup) servings

Chicken 'N Orange Salad

TOMATO MUSHROOM SALAD 🌀

6 large fresh .... Position **Disc** in **Bowl** with
  mushrooms **slicing side up.** Slice
4 medium tomatoes, mushrooms (page 33) and
  cored, halved tomatoes. Empty **Bowl** as
  sliced vegetables reach
  Fill Level. Transfer to salad
  bowl.

2 tablespoons olive oil ... Add olive oil, lemon juice
2 teaspoons lemon and basil to salad bowl.
  juice Salt and pepper to taste.
1 teaspoon basil Marinate at least 1 hour.
  Salt and pepper Toss and serve over lettuce
  leaves.

Makes 6 (¾-cup) servings

VARIATION:
Fresh Vegetable Salad: Slice 1 small red onion, 1 medium cucumber and 1 medium zucchini. Add to mushrooms and tomatoes. Increase oil to ¼ cup and lemon
juice to 2 tablespoons. Marinate as directed above.
Makes 12 (¾-cup) servings.

CARROT RAISIN TOSS 🌑🌒

Make this nutritious salad in any quantity. When preparing large amounts, remember to empty Bowl as carrots reach Fill Level.

2 large carrots, ... **peeled, cut in 2-inch pieces**	Position **Disc** in **Bowl** with **shredding side up.** Stack carrots horizontally in food chute. Shred. Remove to serving dish.
½ cup raisins . . . . **4 tablespoons mayonnaise (page 100) or salad dressing**	Add remaining ingredients and toss.

Makes 2 (¾-cup) servings

SHORT CUT WALDORF SALAD 🌒

½ cup walnuts . . . . **3 large stalks celery, each cut crosswise in thirds** **6 medium apples, quartered, cored**	Position **Disc** in **Bowl** with **slicing side up.** Slice walnuts and celery. Transfer to large mixing bowl. Slice half the apples, add to mixing bowl. Repeat with remaining apples and add to mixing bowl.
½ cup raisins . . . . **½ cup mayonnaise (page 100)**	Add raisins and mayonnaise. Mix well, making sure apples are coated with mayonnaise. Serve on lettuce leaves.

Makes 10 (¾-cup) servings

MUSHROOM SPINACH SALAD 🌑🌒

8 ounces fresh . . . . **spinach, cleaned, torn in bite-size pieces**	Place spinach in extra large salad bowl; set aside.
2 ounces Parmesan or Romano cheese	Position **Disc** in **Bowl** with **shredding side up.** Shred cheese; add to spinach.
4 ounces fresh . . . . **mushrooms**	Position **Disc** in **Bowl** with **slicing side up;** slice mushrooms (page 33). Add to spinach.
⅓ to ½ cup Oil and . . . . **Vinegar Dressing (page 101)** **Salt and pepper**	Just before serving, toss with dressing. Salt and pepper to taste. Sprinkle with croutons if desired.

Makes about 8 (1-cup) servings

Top to bottom:
Short Cut Waldorf Salad
Fresh Spicy Salad
Mushroom Spinach Salad

Overnight Cabbage Slaw

FRESH SPICY SALAD 😋

1 cucumber, halved crosswise and lengthwise 1 medium green pepper, quartered 1 small onion, halved 2 medium stalks celery, each cut crosswise in thirds 2 medium tomatoes, halved	Position **Disc** in **Bowl** with **slicing side up**; slice vegetables. As sliced food reaches Fill Level, empty into mixing bowl.
3 tablespoons vinegar 1 tablespoon vegetable oil 1 teaspoon sugar 1 teaspoon salt ¼ teaspoon chili powder Dash hot pepper sauce	Add vinegar, oil, sugar and seasonings to mixing bowl. Toss and refrigerate until serving time. Drain before serving.

Makes 6 (¾-cup) servings

OVERNIGHT CABBAGE SLAW 😋⚙️〜

½ medium cabbage, cut in wedges 1 small sweet or red onion, halved ½ medium green pepper	Position **Disc** in **Bowl** with **slicing side up**; slice cabbage, onion and pepper. When vegetables reach Fill Level, transfer to extra large bowl and slice remaining quantity.
2 carrots, peeled	Position **Disc** in **Bowl** with **shredding side up**; shred carrots. Add to cabbage mixture.
⅔ cup vinegar ⅓ cup vegetable oil ¼ cup sugar 1 teaspoon salt ¼ teaspoon pepper	Position **Knife Blade** in **Bowl.** Add vinegar, oil, sugar, salt and pepper. Process until well mixed, about 10 seconds. Pour over vegetables; stir to combine.

Cover; refrigerate at least 8 hours before serving. At serving time, stir thoroughly; then drain.

Makes 6 (1-cup) servings

NOTE: May be made a day or two in advance.

Fruited Lemon Mold

FRUITED LEMON MOLD 😊

1 package (3-oz.) lemon gelatin 1 cup boiling water	. . . . .Stir gelatin into boiling water until dissolved.
1 cup cold water	. . . . .Stir in cold water. Chill in refrigerator until partially set, about 20 minutes.
1 pint fresh strawberries, hulled (page 43) 2 medium bananas (page 20)	. . . . .Position **Disc** in **Bowl** with **slicing side up;** slice strawberries and bananas. As sliced fruit reaches Fill Level, empty into gelatin. Stir to mix fruit into gelatin.

Pour gelatin into 6-cup mold or 1½-quart casserole. Refrigerate until firm. To serve, unmold onto bed of lettuce leaves.

Makes 8 (½-cup) servings

CREAMY MANDARIN SALAD 😊

1 package (3-oz.) orange gelatin 1 cup boiling water	. . . . . . .Stir gelatin into boiling water until dissolved.
1 cup cold water	. . . . .Stir in cold water. Chill in refrigerator until partially set, about 40 minutes.
1 cup sour cream ½ cup shredded coconut	. . . . . . .Stir sour cream and coconut into partially set gelatin.
1 cup pecans or walnuts	. . . . .Position **Knife Blade** in **Bowl;** add pecans; Pulse to chop coarsely, about 3 to 4 seconds. Add to gelatin mixture.
2 small bananas (page 20) 1 can (11-oz.) mandarin orange segments, drained	. . . . .Position **Disc** in **Bowl** with **slicing side up;** slice bananas; add to gelatin mixture along with orange segments.

Gently stir banana slices and orange segments into gelatin mixture. Pour mixture into 5-cup mold or serving dish. Refrigerate until firm. To serve, unmold onto bed of lettuce leaves, if desired.

Makes 8 (½-cup) servings

COTTAGE CHEESE CALICO SALAD 👁🔲

This festive luncheon salad is refreshing and easy on the waistline.

2 envelopes . . . . In 1-quart saucepan soft-
unflavored gelatin en gelatin in milk, about 10
1 cup milk minutes; then heat until
dissolved over low heat.
Cool to lukewarm.

1 medium stalk celery, . . . Position **Knife Blade** in
cut in 1-inch pieces **Bowl**; add celery, green
½ medium green pepper and green onions
pepper, cut in to **Bowl.** Pulse to chop
6 pieces medium coarse. Transfer
3 green onions, cut to large mixing bowl. Re-
in 1-inch pieces peat for carrot and radish-
1 carrot, peeled, cut es; add to mixing bowl.
in 1-inch pieces Then with cucumber; add
6 radishes, halved to mixing bowl.
½ medium cucumber,
halved lengthwise,
cut in 1-inch pieces

1 container (16-oz.) . . . . . In **Blender Jar,** combine
creamed cottage cottage cheese, mayon-
cheese naise, lemon juice, vinegar,
½ cup mayonnaise horseradish, salt and gela-
2 tablespoons lemon tin mixture. Blend at Liquefy
juice speed just to mix ingredi-
2 tablespoons vinegar ents together, about 5 to
1 to 2 teaspoons 10 seconds. Stir into chop-
prepared ped vegetables. Pour into
horseradish 6-cup mold. Refrigerate
1 teaspoon seasoned until set. Unmold onto bed
salt of greens and garnish with
parsley.

Makes 1 (5-cup) mold,
about 6 (¾-cup) servings

ORANGE DELIGHT SALAD 🔅

1 package (3-oz.) . . . . Stir gelatin into boiling
orange gelatin water until dissolved.
1 cup boiling water

½ cup cold water . . . . Add cold water. Chill until
gelatin is partially set,
about 35 minutes.

2 large carrots, peeled, . . . Position **Disc** in **Bowl** with
cut in 2-inch pieces **shredding side up;** shred
carrots. Add to gelatin.

1 can (8½-oz.) . . . . Stir in pineapple and raisins.
unsweetened
crushed pineapple,
undrained
½ cup raisins

Pour gelatin mixture into 4-cup mold or 1½-quart casserole. Refrigerate until firm. To serve, unmold onto bed of
greens.

Makes 6 (½-cup) servings

CRUNCHY TOMATO ASPIC 👁

2 envelopes . . . . Sprinkle gelatin over cold
unflavored gelatin water in 1½-quart sauce-
1 cup cold water pan. Dissolve over low heat.

1 small clove garlic, ... Stir in garlic, tomato juice,
peeled, minced lemon juice, sugar and
(page 15) seasonings. Chill gelatin
2 cups tomato juice mixture until partially set,
¼ cup lemon juice about 40 minutes.
1 tablespoon sugar
1 teaspoon salt
Dash hot pepper sauce
Dash pepper

1 medium stalk celery, . . . Position **Knife Blade** in
cut in 1-inch pieces **Bowl.** Add celery, onion
1 small onion, quartered and pepper. Pulse to chop
½ green pepper, cut coarsely. Stir into partially
in 6 pieces set gelatin. Repeat with
½ cucumber, cut in cucumber.
1-inch pieces

Pour into 5-cup mold or serving bowl and refrigerate until
set. Unmold on lettuce leaves before serving, if desired.

Makes 8 (½-cup) servings

Crunchy Tomato Aspic

HOW TO MAKE HOMEMADE MAYONNAISE ✎

Position Knife Blade in Bowl. Add egg, ⅓ cup oil, vinegar, sugar and seasonings. Process for 5 seconds.

Pour remaining ⅔ cup oil in a steady stream through food chute with the Processor running.

Process only until mixture is thick and smooth, about 10 seconds.

HOMEMADE MAYONNAISE ✎

1 egg	Position **Knife Blade** in dry **Bowl**. (Recipe won't work unless **Bowl** is dry!) Add all ingredients and process 5 seconds.
⅓ cup vegetable oil	
2 tablespoons vinegar*	
1 teaspoon sugar	
½ teaspoon dry mustard	
½ teaspoon salt	
⅔ cup vegetable oil	Quickly add oil in a steady stream through food chute with Processor running. After all oil is added, process only until mixture is thick and smooth, about 10 seconds.

Makes 1¼ cups

*Use a light vinegar such as white, or use lemon juice.

MUSTARD MAYONNAISE ✎

1 recipe Homemade Mayonnaise (above)	Position **Knife Blade** in **Bowl**. Prepare mayonnaise as directed; then add remaining ingredients and process 5 seconds.
1 tablespoon Dijon-style mustard	
1 tablespoon capers, drained	
½ teaspoon chopped chives	
¼ teaspoon tarragon	

Makes 1 cup

THOUSAND ISLAND DRESSING ✎

1 recipe Homemade Mayonnaise (opposite)	Position **Knife Blade** in **Bowl**. Prepare mayonnaise as directed; then add remaining ingredients and process until finely chopped but not smooth, about 15 seconds. Stop to scrape down sides of **Bowl** once while processing.
¼ cup chili sauce	
1 hard-cooked egg, quartered	
1 medium sweet or dill pickle, quartered	
¼ green pepper, cut in thirds	
1 teaspoon instant minced onion	
¼ teaspoon paprika	

Makes 2 cups

GREEN GODDESS DRESSING ✎

1 recipe Homemade Mayonnaise (above)	Position **Knife Blade** in **Bowl**. Prepare mayonnaise as directed; then add remaining ingredients and process until finely chopped, but not smooth, about 10 seconds.
½ cup sour cream	
1 can (2-oz.) anchovy fillets, drained	
2 sprigs parsley	
1 tablespoon lemon juice	
1 teaspoon instant minced onion	
⅛ teaspoon garlic powder	
Dash pepper	
3 drops green food coloring	

Makes 2 cups

CELERY SEED DRESSING 🐚

1 cup vegetable oil
⅓ cup vinegar
¼ cup confectioners' sugar
1 teaspoon celery seed
1 teaspoon dry mustard
1 teaspoon instant minced onion
1 teaspoon salt

Position **Knife Blade** in **Bowl;** add all ingredients. Process until well mixed, about 10 seconds. Refrigerate until ready to use.

Makes about 1¼ cups

SPECIAL VINAIGRETTE DRESSING ▽

1 cup vegetable oil
1 small stalk celery, cut in 4 pieces
¼ small green pepper, cut in thirds
4 sprigs parsley
1 to 2 tablespoons vinegar
1 teaspoon salt
1 teaspoon tarragon
½ teaspoon instant minced onion
¼ teaspoon dry mustard

Combine all ingredients in **Blender Jar.** Cover; blend at Puree speed until vegetables are finely chopped, about 30 seconds.

Makes about 1⅓ cups

OIL AND VINEGAR DRESSING ▽

¾ cup vegetable oil
¼ cup vinegar
½ teaspoon salt
Dash pepper

Combine ingredients in **Blender Jar.** Cover and blend at Blend speed for 10 seconds.

VARIATION:
Garlic-Herb Dressing: Add ½ teaspoon of your favorite herb and a pinch of garlic powder.

Makes about 1 cup

FRENCH DRESSING ▽

½ cup vegetable oil
⅓ cup chili sauce or catsup
⅓ cup sugar
¼ cup vinegar
1 small clove garlic, peeled
½ teaspoon celery seed
½ teaspoon salt
¼ teaspoon instant minced onion

Combine all ingredients in **Blender Jar.** Cover; blend at Puree speed until ingredients are well blended, about 10 seconds.

Makes about 1 cup

VINEGAR FOR CALORIE COUNTERS ▽

¼ cup wine vinegar
¼ cup water
1 clove garlic, peeled
1 teaspoon sugar
¼ teaspoon salt
¼ teaspoon paprika

Place all ingredients in **Blender Jar.** Cover; blend at Blend speed until garlic is finely chopped, about 30 seconds.

Makes ½ cup

CREAMY ROQUEFORT DRESSING 🐚

1 package (8-oz.) cream cheese, chilled, cut in 6 pieces
½ cup mayonnaise
½ teaspoon garlic salt
½ cup milk

Position **Knife Blade** in **Bowl.** Add cream cheese, mayonnaise and garlic salt. Pulse until smooth, about 15 seconds. Pour milk through food chute with Processor running.

4 ounces Roquefort or blue cheese, broken in 1-inch cubes

Add cheese to **Bowl.** Pulse 10 to 20 seconds to mix in cheese; Pulse longer for a smoother consistency.

Makes 2 cups

Creamy Roquefort Dressing

Savory

Sauces & Butters

A sauce can dress up a simple meal or dessert, and turn leftovers into something special. Sauces are a secret of gourmet cooking. They're versatile, too; often you can create a new sauce by changing one ingredient.

Let the Food Processor slice, chop or shred ingredients for hearty sauces, and homogenize or smooth subtle ones. Try using flavored butters to add distinction to main dishes, vegetables and sandwiches.

MARINARA SAUCE ❧

This hearty Italian sauce may be served hot or cold with chicken, pork, meatloaf, fish, souffles and pasta.

⅓ cup olive or vegetable oil	In 3-quart saucepan heat oil over medium high heat.
1 large clove garlic, peeled **2 medium onions, quartered** **4 sprigs parsley**	Position **Knife Blade** in **Bowl.** Drop garlic through food chute with Processor running. Turn off. Add onions and parsley to **Bowl.** Pulse to chop finely. Add to saucepan and sauté.
1 large green pepper, cut in 12 pieces	Position **Knife Blade** in **Bowl.** Add pepper; Pulse to chop coarsely. Add to onions and continue sautéing over medium high heat, about 10 minutes.
3 cans (1-lb. each) whole tomatoes	Position **Knife Blade** in **Bowl;** add 1 can tomatoes. Pulse to chop coarsely, 1 to 2 seconds. Add to vegetables. Repeat with remaining tomatoes.
1 tablespoon sugar **2 teaspoons salt** **½ teaspoon oregano** **¼ teaspoon pepper**	Stir in seasonings. Simmer, uncovered, until thick, about 2 hours. Sauce may be refrigerated 3 or 4 days, or frozen.

Makes 6 cups

VARIATION:
Italian Spaghetti Sauce: Brown 1 pound ground beef or meatballs in 12-inch skillet. Add 2 cups sauce and 1 can (8-oz.) tomato sauce. Simmer 15 minutes. Serve over hot cooked spaghetti. Makes 6 cups spaghetti sauce.

Italian Spaghetti Sauce,
A Marinara Sauce variation

PESTO ⊕〜

Pesto is a specialty from Genoa, Italy. Toss it with 8 ounces hot, cooked and drained spaghetti or noodles. Pesto keeps well in the freezer.

4 ounces Parmesan cheese **6 sprigs parsley** **1 clove garlic, peeled**	Grate cheese as directed on page 14. Remove **Disc** from **Bowl.** Keep **Knife Blade** in place. Add parsley and garlic to cheese in **Bowl.** Process to finely chop, about 15 to 20 seconds.
⅓ cup pine nuts or walnuts* **¼ cup olive or vegetable oil** **½ teaspoon basil** **¼ teaspoon salt**	Add remaining ingredients. Process to mix and finely chop, about 20 seconds.

Makes about 1¼ cups

*One package (10-oz.) frozen chopped spinach, cooked and squeezed dry, may be substituted for the nuts.

VELOUTÉ SAUCE 〜

5 sprigs parsley	Position dry **Knife Blade** in dry **Bowl.** Add parsley. Pulse to chop finely.
4 tablespoons butter or margarine **4 tablespoons all-purpose flour**	In 1-quart saucepan melt butter over medium heat. Add parsley and sauté for 1 minute; then stir in flour.
1 can (10¾-oz.) condensed chicken broth or consommé **Salt and pepper to taste**	Add broth; cook, stirring constantly, until thickened. Add seasonings. Serve with chicken or fish dishes.

Makes 1⅔ cups

CUCUMBER SAUCE ⊕

½ small cucumber, unpeeled, seeded (page 28)	Position **Disc** in **Bowl** with **shredding side up;** shred cucumber. Transfer to small mixing bowl.
1 cup sour cream **1 teaspoon dill weed** **1 teaspoon instant minced onion** **Salt and pepper to taste**	Add remaining ingredients to shredded cucumber and mix together. Refrigerate until serving. Serve with tuna, salmon, seafood and other fish.

Makes about 1 cup

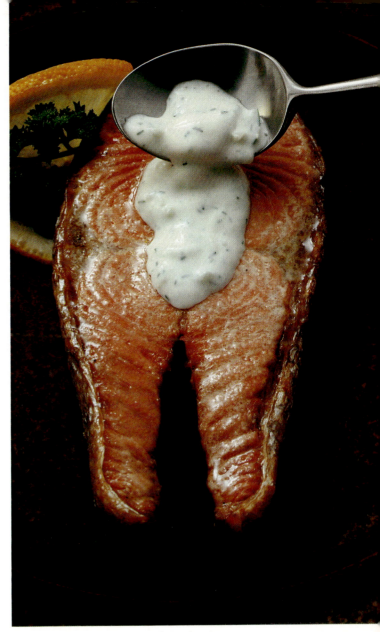

Cucumber Sauce on Salmon Steak

FRESH MUSHROOM SAUCE ⌇

8 ounces fresh mushrooms	Position **Disc** in **Bowl,** with **slicing side up;** slice mushrooms (page 33). Empty **Bowl** when mushrooms reach Fill Level.
¼ cup butter or margarine	In 10-inch skillet melt butter over medium heat. Add mushrooms and sauté for 1 or 2 minutes. Cover; simmer 5 minutes.
¼ cup all-purpose flour **1 can (10½-oz.) beef broth or consommé**	Stir in flour. Add broth slowly, stirring until sauce thickens and is smooth.
½ cup cream or milk **¼ teaspoon salt** **Dash pepper and nutmeg**	Stir in cream and seasonings. Serve hot with meat, poultry or fish.

Makes 2½ cups

HOW TO MAKE HOLLANDAISE SAUCE

Add egg yolks, lemon juice and seasonings to Blender Jar. Cover. Blend at Liquefy speed 3 to 5 seconds.

Heat butter until very hot and bubbling. Remove lid insert; pour in butter with Blender running. Partially shield opening, (see recipe below).

Serve hollandaise sauce hot with meat, poultry, fish or vegetables.

HOLLANDAISE SAUCE

3 egg yolks	.Add egg yolks, lemon juice,
2 tablespoons lemon juice	salt and hot pepper sauce to **Blender Jar.** Cover.
¼ teaspoon salt	
Dash hot pepper sauce	
½ cup butter	.In small saucepan melt butter until very hot and bubbling.

Blend egg yolk mixture at Liquefy speed about 5 seconds. Remove lid insert with Blender running and pour in bubbling butter in steady stream. Partially shield opening with lid insert to prevent butter spattering. Blend until thickened, about 30 seconds. Serve immediately over asparagus, broccoli, poached eggs or salmon.

Makes ¾ cup

CHEDDAR CHEESE SAUCE

4 ounces natural	.Position **Disc** in **Bowl** with
Cheddar cheese	**shredding side up;** shred cheese. Leave in **Bowl.**
2 tablespoons butter	.In 1-quart saucepan melt
or margarine	butter over low heat. Stir in
2 tablespoons all-purpose flour	flour.
1 cup milk	.Add milk; cook over medium high heat, stirring constantly, until thickened. Remove from heat.
¼ teaspoon salt	.Stir in cheese and salt.

Makes 1⅓ cups

HONEY WALNUT GLAZE

½ cup walnuts	.Position **Knife Blade** in **Bowl;** add walnuts. Process 5 seconds.
½ cup honey	.Combine honey and walnuts in 2-cup measuring cup; stir to mix.

Spread on ham or poultry the last half hour of baking.

Makes ¾ cup

BEARNAISE SAUCE

1 recipe Hollandaise	.Prepare Hollandaise Sauce
Sauce (above)	as directed in recipe and leave in **Blender Jar.**
1 green onion, cut in	.Position **Knife Blade** in dry
1-inch pieces	**Bowl;** add parsley and on-
2 sprigs parsley	ion pieces. Process to mince. Empty into 1-quart saucepan.
2 tablespoons white	.Add wine, tarragon vinegar,
wine	dried tarragon and pepper
2 teaspoons tarragon	to saucepan. Cook over
vinegar	medium heat until about 1
1 teaspoon dried	teaspoon of liquid remains.
tarragon	Add to Hollandaise Sauce
Dash pepper	in **Blender Jar.**

Cover and blend at Blend speed for about 10 seconds. Serve immediately over broiled meats. Refrigerate leftover sauce; reheat in a double boiler.

Makes 1 cup

TARTAR SAUCE ～

| 1 recipe Homemade Mayonnaise (page 100) | Position **Knife Blade** in **Bowl.** Prepare mayonnaise as directed; then add remaining ingredients and process until finely chopped but not smooth, about 10 seconds. |

1 recipe Homemade
   Mayonnaise
   (page 100)
1 medium dill or
   sweet pickle,
   quartered
2 sprigs parsley
1 tablespoon capers,
   drained
1 tablespoon lemon
   juice
1 teaspoon instant
   minced onion
¼ teaspoon
   Worcestershire
   sauce

Position **Knife Blade** in **Bowl.** Prepare mayonnaise as directed; then add remaining ingredients and process until finely chopped but not smooth, about 10 seconds.

Makes 1½ cups

Zippy Pepper Butter

BUTTERY GARLIC TOPPING ～

½ cup butter or
   margarine, chilled,
   cut in 8 pieces
4 sprigs parsley
1 clove garlic, peeled
1 teaspoon
   Worcestershire
   sauce
½ teaspoon dry
   mustard
¼ teaspoon pepper

Position **Knife Blade** in **Bowl.** Add all ingredients. Process about 20 to 30 seconds, Pulsing several times, until mixture is combined. Scrape mixture down from sides of **Bowl** if necessary and process 5 to 10 seconds longer. Spread mixture over steaks, hamburgers or chicken during broiling.

Cover unused topping tightly and refrigerate.

Makes ½ cup

ZIPPY PEPPER BUTTER ～

1 small clove garlic,
   peeled
4 sprigs parsley
¼ small green pepper,
   cut in thirds

Position **Knife Blade** in **Bowl;** add parsley. Drop garlic through food chute with Processor running. Turn off. Add green pepper; Pulse to chop finely, 4 to 5 seconds. Scrape down sides of **Bowl.**

½ cup soft butter
   or margarine, cut
   in 6 pieces
¼ teaspoon salt
2 drops hot pepper
   sauce

Add butter and seasonings; distribute evenly. Process until mixed, about 20 to 30 seconds. Scrape down sides of **Bowl** 1 or 2 times, if necessary.

Serve with steak, hamburgers or baked potatoes.

Makes about ½ cup

HOMEMADE BUTTER ～

1 cup well-chilled
   heavy cream, about
   a week old
2 to 3 drops yellow
   food coloring
   (optional, use for a
   deeper color)

Position **Knife Blade** in **Bowl;** add cream including thick cream that may have formed on sides of carton. Process until butter forms into ball, 2 to 5 minutes, depending on age of cream. Drain butter in a colander, then place in bowl and press out remaining liquid with wooden spoon.

If desired, add ½ teaspoon salt. Place in crock or dish and refrigerate. Keeps 1 week.

Makes about ½ cup

VARIATION:
For flavored butter, add 1 small clove garlic, ½ teaspoon onion salt or garlic powder or ½ teaspoon of your favorite ground herb or spice to cream and process as above.

PARMESAN BUTTER ～ 🌀

2 ounces Parmesan
   cheese*

Position **Knife Blade** in **Bowl** with **Disc** above it, **shredding side up.** Grate cheese (page 14).

½ cup soft butter or
   margarine, chilled,
   cut in 8 pieces
3 sprigs parsley
½ teaspoon onion
   powder
   Dash hot pepper
   sauce

Remove **Disc** from **Bowl.** Add butter, distributing evenly, parsley, onion powder and hot pepper sauce. Pulse until well mixed, about 40 seconds. Stop several times and scrape down sides of **Bowl.**

Makes ⅔ cup

*Natural Cheddar cheese (2-oz.), shredded in Processor, may be substituted for Parmesan.

Plain & Fancy
Vegetables

We all know that vegetables play an important role in sound nutrition, but some people need to be coaxed to eat their vegetables. Perhaps they're tired of the 'same old thing.' Be imaginative with vegetables!

Buy vegetables in season; they cost less because they're plentiful, and taste best because they're at the peak of flavor and freshness. The Food Processor helps you provide variety. Chop them, slice them, shred them or sauce them. Vegetables need never be dull.

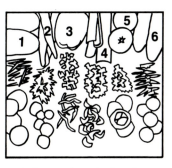

1. Julienned and sliced potatoes, page 15, 41
2. Shredded and sliced carrots, page 12, 16
3. Chopped and sliced peppers, page 38, 39
4. Chopped and sliced celery, page 24, 23
5. Chopped and sliced onions, page 14, 35
6. Julienned and sliced zucchini, page 15, 16

Crumb-Topped Celery Bake

CRUMB-TOPPED CELERY BAKE ●

8 medium stalks	.........Preheat oven to 375°F. Po-
celery, each cut	sition **Disc** in **Bowl** with
crosswise in thirds	**slicing side up;** slice cel-
1 can (8-oz.) water	ery and water chestnuts.
chestnuts, drained	When sliced vegetables

reach Fill Level, empty **Bowl** into ungreased, shallow, 1½-quart casserole. Slice remaining vegetables.

1 can (10¾-oz.) ....Add soup to casserole; stir
condensed cream to mix.
of chicken soup

½ cup Toasty ....Sprinkle crumbs over cel-
Seasoned Bread ery mixture. Bake for 45
Crumbs (opposite) minutes.

Makes 6 (½-cup) servings

TASTY SLICED CARROTS ●

8 medium carrots, ...Position **Disc** in **Bowl** with
peeled (page 12) **slicing side up;** slice carrots. As carrots reach Fill Level, empty into large mixing bowl.

¾ cup water ....In 2-quart saucepan com-
1 teaspoon salt bine water and salt. Bring to a boil; add carrots. Cover and simmer until carrots are tender, about 15 to 20 minutes. Drain.

¼ cup milk ....Quickly stir in milk, butter,
2 tablespoons butter dill weed and nutmeg.
½ teaspoon dill weed Serve hot.
¼ teaspoon nutmeg

Makes 4 (¾-cup) servings

CARAWAY BUTTERED CABBAGE ●

½ medium cabbage, ...Position **Disc** in **Bowl** with
cut in wedges **slicing side up;** slice cabbage. As cabbage reaches Fill Level, transfer to mixing bowl; slice remainder.

2 tablespoons ....In 12-inch skillet heat oil
vegetable oil and butter over high heat.
2 tablespoons butter Add cabbage, caraway
1 teaspoon caraway seeds and salt. Stir-fry for
seeds 3 to 5 minutes.
½ teaspoon salt

2 tablespoons water .....Lower heat; add water.
Cover; cook 5 minutes.

Makes 6 (½-cup) servings

TOASTY SEASONED BREAD CRUMBS ●

4 slices fresh bread, ...Position **Disc** in **Bowl** with
folded in half **shredding side up;** shred
(page 14) bread. Remove **Disc** and
⅛ teaspoon salt stir in seasonings with a
⅛ teaspoon garlic salt spoon.
or powder
Pinch of 3 or 4 herbs
(thyme, basil,
oregano, parsley)

2 tablespoons butter .....In a 12-inch skillet melt
or margarine butter over medium heat.

Add bread mixture. Toast about 3 minutes, stirring often. Cool and put in tightly covered container. Use as needed on tops of casseroles or as a meat coating. Keeps a month in the refrigerator.

Makes 1 cup crumbs

NOTE: Recipe can be doubled. Toast in a 12-inch or electric skillet for about 5 minutes.

Green Onion Custard Pie

CREAMED ONIONS AND MUSHROOMS 🐟🐑

1 slice fresh bread, ... **any kind, folded in half (page 14)**	Preheat oven to 375°F. Position **Disc** in **Bowl** with **shredding side up.** Shred bread; set aside in small mixing bowl.
4 medium onions, ... **halved**	Position **Disc** in **Bowl** with **slicing side up.** Slice onions and transfer to 8-inch square baking pan.
4 ounces fresh . . . . **mushrooms**	Position **Disc** in **Bowl** with **slicing side up.** Slice mushrooms and spread over onions.
1 can (10¾-oz.) . . . . **condensed cream of celery soup Pepper Butter**	Spread cream of celery soup over mushrooms and top with bread crumbs. Sprinkle with pepper and dot with butter. Bake for 30 minutes.

Makes 6 (½-cup) servings

GREEN BEANS ORIENTAL 🐑

4 large stalks celery, ... **each cut crosswise in thirds**	Position **Disc** in **Bowl** with **slicing side up.** Slice celery.
3 tablespoons butter . . . . . **or margarine**	In 1½-quart saucepan melt butter. When hot, add celery; sauté 2 to 3 minutes.
1 teaspoon salt . . . . **1 package (10-oz.) frozen green beans**	Add salt and beans; stir occasionally until beans are separated. Cover; lower heat; and cook until beans are done and celery is crisp, about 7 minutes. (If needed, add a little water.)

Makes 4 (½-cup) servings

GREEN ONION CUSTARD PIE 🐑🐚

1 9-inch unbaked pie . . . . . **crust (pages 138 & 139)**	Prepare pie crust. Preheat oven to 425°F. Place a piece of aluminum foil over pie crust in pan and fill with dry beans or rice to weigh down pastry and prevent it from puffing as it bakes. Bake for 10 minutes. Remove foil and beans.
4 bunches green . . . . **onions,* about 24 (page 36)**	Position **Disc** in **Bowl** with **slicing side up.** Wedge onions upright in food chute; slice. Empty **Bowl** as onions reach Fill Level.
3 tablespoons butter or . . . **margarine**	In 10-inch skillet melt butter over low heat. Sauté onions in butter until soft. Spread over hot, partially baked pie crust.
2 eggs . . . . **1 cup milk 1 teaspoon salt Dash pepper**	Position **Knife Blade** in **Bowl;** add eggs, milk, salt and pepper. Process until mixed, about 5 seconds.

Pour over onions. Sprinkle surface with shredded cheese, if desired. Bake for 20 to 25 minutes, or until well browned, and knife inserted halfway between center and edge comes out clean.

Makes 1 (9-inch) pie
(about 8 servings)

*Substitute 5 or 6 leeks, including tender green parts, for onions, if desired.

VARIATION:
Caraway Onion Pie: Slice 3 medium onions, cut to fit food chute in Processor, and substitute for green onions. Add 1 teaspoon caraway seed to onion mixture.

WILD RICE VEGETABLE CASSEROLE 🌶

½ cup wild rice, uncooked	Cook rice as directed on package.
4 ounces fresh mushrooms 2 medium stalks celery, each cut crosswise in thirds 1 can (8-oz.) water chestnuts, drained 1 small onion	Position **Disc** in **Bowl** with **slicing side up;** slice vegetables. Empty **Bowl** as slices reach Fill Level.
¼ cup butter or margarine ½ teaspoon salt ⅛ teaspoon pepper	In 10-inch skillet melt butter. Sauté vegetables until soft. Stir in wild rice, salt and pepper. Cover and heat slowly, stirring once or twice, about 10 minutes. Makes 8 (½-cup) servings

NOTE: This wild rice mixture makes an excellent stuffing for duck, cornish hens or other fowl.

CHINESE FRIED RICE 🌶 🌶

2 ounces fresh mushrooms, about 3 or 4 2 medium stalks celery, cut in 1-inch pieces 6 green onions, cut in 1-inch pieces 1 cup cooked chicken, shrimp, pork or beef, cut in 1-inch cubes	Position **Knife Blade** in **Bowl** with **Disc** above it, **slicing side up.** Process mushrooms; empty into medium size bowl. Position **Knife Blade** in **Bowl** and process celery, onions and meat separately, Pulsing to chop coarsely. Empty each into bowl with mushrooms.
2 eggs	Position **Knife Blade** in **Bowl;** add eggs and process to blend, 2 to 3 Pulses.
4 tablespoons vegetable oil (divided) 2 tablespoons soy sauce	In 12-inch skillet or wok heat 1 tablespoon oil over medium heat. Stir-fry eggs until softly scrambled; remove to dish. Add 2 tablespoons oil and soy sauce. Stir-fry vegetable mixture, 1 to 2 minutes.
2 cups cooked, cold rice (preferably day-old) ¼ teaspoon salt	Add remaining oil and rice; heat thoroughly. Add eggs and salt, stir-fry until hot, about 1 minute. Serve with additional soy sauce. Makes 4 (1-cup) servings

MUSHROOM-RICE PILAF 🌶

8 ounces fresh mushrooms 1 medium onion, halved	Position **Disc** in **Bowl** with **slicing side up.** Slice mushrooms (page 33) and onion.
4 tablespoons butter	In 12-inch skillet melt butter over moderate heat. Add mushrooms and onion and sauté until soft.
2 cups quick-cooking rice 1⅔ cups water 2 chicken bouillon cubes, crushed 1 teaspoon salt 1 bay leaf ½ teaspoon pepper	Add rice, water, bouillon cubes, salt, bay leaf and pepper. Bring to a vigorous boil. Cover; reduce heat and simmer until water is absorbed and rice is tender, about 5 to 10 minutes. Makes 8 (¾-cup) servings

Mushroom-Rice Pilaf

Stir-Fry Vegetable Medley

STIR-FRY VEGETABLE MEDLEY 🍲

2 firm medium tomatoes, halved	Position **Disc** in **Bowl** with **slicing side up;** slice tomatoes. Set aside in small bowl.
2 medium stalks celery, each cut crosswise in thirds **1 medium zucchini, halved** **1 small onion, quartered** **½ green pepper**	Slice celery, zucchini, onion and green pepper. Empty **Bowl** as vegetables reach Fill Level.
3 tablespoons vegetable oil	In 12-inch skillet or wok heat oil over high heat. Add all sliced vegetables, except tomatoes; stir-fry until not quite tender, about 2 minutes.
1 package (10-oz.) frozen corn, partially defrosted **1 tablespoon butter** **1 teaspoon salt** **Dash pepper**	Stir in corn, butter and seasonings. Cover; simmer until corn is tender, 4 to 5 minutes. Do not overcook. Add tomatoes and stir into hot vegetables; serve immediately.

Makes 10 (½-cup) servings

TOMATO-ZUCCHINI CASSEROLE 🍲

4 small zucchini **4 tomatoes, halved** **2 green peppers, halved**	Preheat oven to 350°F. Position **Disc** in **Bowl** with **slicing side up;** slice vegetables. Empty **Bowl** when sliced vegetables reach Fill Level. Spread half of the sliced vegetables in a 2-quart baking dish.
Basil leaves (optional) **6 slices American cheese**	Sprinkle with ½ teaspoon basil leaves. Cover with 3 slices cheese. Add remaining vegetables. Sprinkle with ½ teaspoon basil leaves; cover with remaining cheese.
2 tablespoons butter	Dot surface with butter.

Cover and bake until zucchini is tender, about 45 minutes.

Makes 8 (¾-cup) servings

Cheesy Scalloped Potatoes

CHEESY SCALLOPED POTATOES

8 ounces natural Cheddar cheese	Preheat oven to 350°F. Position **Disc** in **Bowl** with **shredding side up;** shred cheese. Set aside.
¼ cup butter or margarine **¼ cup all-purpose flour**	In 2-quart saucepan melt butter over low heat. Blend in flour.
2 cups milk	Add milk all at once; cook, stirring constantly, until slightly thickened. Add shredded cheese.
1 teaspoon salt **¼ teaspoon pepper**	Season and continue to cook, stirring, until cheese melts. Remove from heat. Spread half the cheese sauce on bottom of shallow, 2½-quart baking dish.
5 medium potatoes,* cut to fit food chute **2 small yellow onions**	Position **Disc** in **Bowl** with **slicing side up;** slice potatoes and onions.

As vegetables reach Fill Level, empty into baking dish. Arrange potato and onion slices over cheese sauce. Spread remaining cheese sauce over top. Bake until potatoes are tender, about 1 hour.

Makes 8 (¾-cup) servings

*Peel potatoes only if desired; they look attractive with the skins on.

CHEESY SPINACH BAKE

2 packages (10-oz. each) frozen chopped spinach **1 cup sour cream** **1 package (about 1.4-oz.) dried onion soup mix**	Cook spinach as directed on package. Drain well and press out excess moisture. Place in large mixing bowl. Add sour cream and soup mix.
4 ounces natural Cheddar cheese, chilled, cut to fit food chute	Preheat oven to 350°F. Position **Disc** in **Bowl** with **shredding side up;** shred cheese. Add to spinach. Mix well and transfer to shallow 2-quart casserole.
2 slices fresh bread **Butter, softened**	Lightly butter bread slices. Fold slices in half with buttered sides together. Position **Disc** in **Bowl** with **shredding side up.** Shred bread. Sprinkle bread crumbs over top of casserole. Bake 20 to 25 minutes.

Makes 6 (½-cup) servings

POTATO PANCAKES

3 eggs	Position **Knife Blade** in **Bowl;** add eggs and process, 5 seconds. Leave **Knife Blade** in **Bowl.**
1 medium onion, quartered **3 medium potatoes, unpeeled, cut to fit food chute**	Add onion to **Bowl.** Position **Disc** above **Knife Blade, shredding side up.** Shred potatoes and continue to process until finely chopped.
2 tablespoons all-purpose flour **1 teaspoon lemon juice** **1 teaspoon salt** **½ teaspoon pepper**	Remove **Disc** from **Bowl;** add flour, lemon juice, salt and pepper. Process 5 seconds.
Vegetable oil	In 10-inch skillet heat small amount of vegetable oil over medium high heat.

Spoon 2 heaping tablespoonfuls of potato mixture into skillet for each pancake. Brown on both sides until done, about 2 to 3 minutes per side. Serve topped with sour cream.

Makes 1 dozen (3½-inch) pancakes

CRISP 'N CRUNCHY DEEP FRY SLICES

Potatoes	Select potatoes that will fit through food chute whole. Scrub well; peel, if desired. Position **Disc** in **Bowl** with **slicing side up**; slice potatoes. Empty **Bowl** as slices reach Fill Level. Pat dry.
Vegetable oil for frying . . .	In 3-quart saucepan, deep electric skillet or deep fat fryer, heat oil to 375°F. Fry slices until golden and tender, about 5 to 8 minutes. Stir occasionally to keep slices from sticking together. Drain on paper towels.
Salt	Sprinkle with salt and serve hot.

1 medium potato makes 2 (¾-cup) servings

SWEET CRUNCHY YAMS

½ cup packed brown sugar . . . . . **¼ cup butter or margarine, chilled** **½ cup pecans**	Preheat oven to 375°F. Position **Knife Blade** in **Bowl**. Add brown sugar, butter and pecans. Pulse until butter is cut into sugar and mixture is crumbly, about 15 seconds. Transfer to small bowl.
1 can (23- to 24-oz.) yams,* drained and quartered	Position **Knife Blade** in **Bowl**. Add half of yam pieces. Pulse until crumbly, about 10 seconds. Spread yams in 9-inch pie pan. Repeat with second half and add to pie pan. Sprinkle pecan mixture over top. Bake 20 to 25 minutes.

Makes 4 (½-cup) servings

*Two cups cooked winter squash can be substituted for canned yams.

WESTERN FRIES (Farm-Style Fries)

This recipe may be doubled or cut in half.

4 medium potatoes, scrubbed, cut to fit food chute	Position **Disc** in **Bowl** with **slicing side up**; slice potatoes. (No need to peel unless desired.) Empty **Bowl** when potato slices reach Fill Level.
4 slices bacon	Fry bacon in skillet. Remove bacon, leave fat in skillet. Fry potato slices in bacon fat over medium heat, turning often, until tender and golden brown. Crumble bacon and sprinkle over top of potatoes.
Salt and pepper	Season to taste.

Makes 4 (¾-cup) servings

Western Fries

SAUTÉED ZUCCHINI 🔵

Parmesan or Romano cheese	Grate cheese following directions on page 14.
1 medium zucchini per serving, cut crosswise in 2-inch pieces Salt	Position **Disc** in **Bowl** with **shredding side up.** Place zucchini pieces horizontally in food chute; shred. Transfer to colander and salt lightly. Let stand 10 minutes. Drain and press or wring out moisture.
2 tablespoons vegetable oil	In 10-inch skillet heat small amount of oil over high heat. Add zucchini and stir-fry until tender, about 2 minutes.
Butter Salt	To serve, dot with butter, salt to taste and sprinkle with Parmesan or Romano cheese.

1 medium zucchini makes 1 (½-cup) serving

DELUXE ZUCCHINI SAUTÉ 🔵 〰

4 medium zucchini 1 teaspoon salt	Position **Disc** in **Bowl** with **shredding side up.** Shred zucchini. When zucchini reaches Fill Level, empty into colander. Sprinkle with salt; let stand 10 minutes. Drain and press or wring out as much liquid as possible. Spread on paper towels and allow to drain further.
1 small onion, quartered	Position **Knife Blade** in **Bowl.** Add onion. Pulse to chop coarsely.
¼ cup butter ¼ teaspoon salt ½ cup sour cream ¼ teaspoon basil	In 10-inch skillet melt butter over medium high heat. Sauté onion for 1 minute. Add zucchini and salt. Cook, stirring occasionally, until just tender, about 6 minutes. Remove from heat. Stir in sour cream and basil. Serve immediately.

Makes 4 (½-cup) servings

HOW TO STUFF EGGPLANT

Halve eggplant lengthwise. Scoop out insides, leaving ½-inch shells. Salt lightly; place in baking dish.

Sauté beef, green pepper and onion. Stir in tomatoes. Chop eggplant pulp, (see recipe, page 115).

Spoon stuffing into eggplant shells. Sprinkle with remaining crumb mixture and bake until tender.

STUFFED EGGPLANT

1 slice fresh bread, quartered 2 sprigs parsley	Position **Knife Blade** in **Bowl.** Add bread and parsley. Process to chop finely, about 10 seconds. Set aside in small mixing bowl.
1 tablespoon vegetable oil ½ pound ground beef	In 10-inch skillet heat oil over medium high heat. Add beef and brown, breaking meat with a fork from time to time.
1 onion, quartered ¼ green pepper, cut in thirds	Position **Knife Blade** in **Bowl.** Add onion and green pepper. Pulse to chop coarsely. Add to beef and sauté.
2 tomatoes, quartered	Position **Knife Blade** in **Bowl.** Add tomatoes and process to chop coarsely. Stir into beef.
1 medium eggplant Salt	Position **Knife Blade** in **Bowl.** Halve eggplant lengthwise. Carefully scoop out insides and add to **Bowl,** leaving two ½-inch thick shells. Sprinkle inside of shells lightly with salt. Set in shallow 1½-quart baking dish and set aside.
1½ teaspoons oregano 1 teaspoon salt ⅛ teaspoon pepper	Pulse to chop eggplant coarsely. Add to beef along with half the bread crumb mixture and seasonings.

Cook 5 minutes longer. Fill eggplant shells with stuffing. Sprinkle remaining bread crumb mixture over tops. Bake until eggplant is tender, about 45 to 50 minutes. Serve hot.

Makes 2 stuffed shells
(about 4 servings)

RATATOUILLE

This classic vegetable casserole combines eggplant and zucchini with seasonings typical of the Riviera.

3 tablespoons olive or vegetable oil	In 12-inch skillet heat oil over medium high heat.
6 sprigs parsley 1 clove garlic	Position **Knife Blade** in **Bowl;** add parsley and process to chop evenly, dropping garlic through food chute with Processor running. Add to skillet and sauté.
3 small onions, cut to fit food chute	Position **Disc** in **Bowl** with **slicing side up;** slice onions. Add to skillet and sauté onion/parsley mixture over medium high heat until onions are soft.
1 small eggplant, cut in strips to fit food chute 3 medium tomatoes, peeled and halved 2 medium zucchini, washed, with ends removed 1 small green pepper, halved	Position **Disc** in **Bowl** with **slicing side up.** Slice eggplant, tomatoes, zucchini and green pepper. Empty sliced vegetables into skillet as vegetables reach Fill Level.
1 teaspoon salt 1 teaspoon sugar ½ teaspoon basil ⅛ teaspoon pepper 2 dashes hot pepper sauce	Add seasonings to vegetables and carefully stir mixture. Cover and simmer 15 minutes. Uncover and simmer 30 minutes more, until vegetables are tender. Serve hot, sprinkled with additional parsley; or chill and serve cold.

Makes 8 (½-cup) servings

Stuffed Eggplant

Sweet & Sour
Relishes & Marmalades

Relishes and marmalades are an American tradition. They dressed up dinner with a touch of sweet or sour. They preserved fruits and vegetables for the cold winter months. They took a lot of preparation.

Now, with the Food Processor to speed chopping, slicing or shredding, you can rival Grandma's pantry with less time and effort.

PICKLE RELISH 🟢 ～

3 large cucumbers	Remove seeds from cucumbers, if tough. Position **Disc** in **Bowl** with **shredding side up.** Shred cucumbers. As shredded cucumbers reach Fill Level, empty **Bowl** into large mixing bowl.
2 medium stalks celery, each cut in 1-inch pieces **1 green pepper, cut in 12 pieces** **1 red pepper, cut in 12 pieces** **1 medium onion, quartered**	Position **Knife Blade** in **Bowl.** Process vegetables separately, Pulsing to chop coarsely. Add vegetables to shredded cucumbers.
3 tablespoons salt **Water**	Sprinkle with salt; then add enough water to cover vegetables and stir. Let stand 1 hour. Drain well.
1½ cups vinegar **1 cup sugar** **1 teaspoon mustard seed**	In 3-quart saucepan combine vinegar, sugar and mustard seed. Bring to a boil and add vegetables.

Simmer, uncovered, for 15 minutes. Place in hot sterilized jars. Cool; then refrigerate. Will keep in refrigerator several weeks.

Makes 5 cups

NOTE: To can, seal sterilized jars tightly with vacuum seal lids and process in hot water bath for 10 minutes, following manufacturer's directions.

Pickle Relish

CRANBERRY FRUIT RELISH

1 medium orange, ...Position **Knife Blade** in
   unpeeled, **Bowl** with **Disc** above it,
   quartered, seeded **shredding side up;** shred
1 large apple, orange and apple.
   unpeeled,
   quartered, cored

2 cups (½ pound) . . . . . . .Remove **Disc.** (Any unpro-
   fresh or frozen and cessed pieces on top of
   thawed cranberries **Disc** can be added to
¾ cup sugar **Bowl.**) Add cranberries
and sugar. Pulse to desired
consistency. Refrigerate
until serving time.

Makes 2½ cups

NOTE: This relish will keep in the refrigerator up to a
week. Serve with poultry or pork.

CORN RELISH

1 green pepper, cut . . . . . .Position **Knife Blade** in
   in 12 pieces **Bowl.** Process vegetables
1 medium onion, separately, Pulsing to chop
   quartered coarsely. Place in 3-quart
saucepan.

1 package (10-oz.) . . . . . .Add remaining ingredients
   frozen corn or 1 to saucepan. Bring to a
   can (16-oz.) kernels, boil; simmer, uncovered,
   drained for 20 minutes. Chill thor-
½ cup chili sauce oughly before serving. Will
¼ cup sugar keep in refrigerator for 2 to
¼ cup vinegar 3 weeks.
1 teaspoon salt
½ teaspoon celery seed

Makes 3 cups

PEPPER RELISH

1 green pepper, cut in . . . .Position **Knife Blade** in
   12 pieces (page 38) **Bowl.** Process vegetables
1 sweet red pepper, separately, Pulsing to chop
   cut in 12 pieces coarsely. Combine chop-
1 large onion, ped vegetables in 2-quart
   quartered saucepan.

¼ cup vinegar . . . . .Add vinegar, sugar and
¼ cup packed brown salt to vegetables and stir.
   sugar
½ teaspoon salt

Bring to a boil; then reduce heat to a simmer and cook,
covered, for 10 minutes. Chill thoroughly before serving.
Will keep in refrigerator several weeks.

Makes 2 cups

NOTE: To can, pack hot relish in sterilized jars; seal
tightly with vacuum seal lids, and process in hot water
bath for 10 minutes, following manufacturer's directions.

Cranberry Fruit Relish

DOWN HOME RELISH ⑤ ∽

12 large cucumbers, peeled, cut in half lengthwise and crosswise	Scoop out seeds if they are tough. Position **Disc** in **Bowl** with **shredding side up.** Shred cucumbers. When shredded cucumbers reach Fill Level, empty into large mixing bowl.
12 medium yellow onions, quartered	Position **Knife Blade** in **Bowl.** Add 2 quartered onions to **Bowl.** Pulse until onions are coarsely chopped. Empty chopped onions into mixing bowl with shredded cucumber. Chop remaining onions, 2 at a time.
1½ tablespoons salt	Stir salt into vegetables; let stand ½ hour. Drain well. Transfer to an 8- to 10-quart heavy pot.
1½ quarts white vinegar **4 cups sugar** **2½ tablespoons celery seed** **2½ tablespoons mustard seed**	Stir in vinegar, sugar, celery seed and mustard seed. Bring to a boil; simmer for ½ hour, stirring occasionally.
2 tablespoons ground mustard **1 tablespoon turmeric**	Stir in spices.
4 tablespoons cornstarch	In small dish, stir together cornstarch and 5 to 6 tablespoons liquid from relish until smooth.

Add mixture to relish. Cook, stirring constantly, until slightly thickened. Pour into sterile jars and seal tightly.

Makes 7 pints

REFRIGERATOR CUCUMBER PICKLES ⑨

6 to 8 medium cucumbers, unpeeled	Select young, firm cucumbers. Position **Disc** in **Bowl** with **slicing side up.** Slice, using firm pressure on food pusher for even slices. Empty into large mixing bowl as cucumbers reach Fill Level.
2 cups vinegar **2 cups sugar** **¼ cup non-iodized salt**	Bring vinegar, sugar and salt to a boil; boil 1 minute. Immediately pour over cucumbers. Pack in sterilized jars; cover and refrigerate at least 1 week before using.

Makes 4 or 5 pints

CARROT RELISH ⑤ ⑨ ∽

6 medium carrots, peeled, cut crosswise in 2½-inch pieces	Position **Disc** in **Bowl** with **shredding side up;** shred carrots. As shredded carrots reach Fill Level, empty **Bowl** into 3-quart saucepan.
6 medium stalks celery, each cut crosswise in thirds	Position **Disc** in **Bowl** with **slicing side up;** slice celery. Add to carrots.
1 green pepper, cut in 12 pieces (page 38)	Position **Knife Blade** in **Bowl;** add pepper. Pulse to chop coarsely. Add to carrots.
1 cup sugar **¾ cup vinegar** **¼ cup water** **1 tablespoon salt** **1 teaspoon celery seed**	Add remaining ingredients to saucepan; bring to a boil. Then reduce heat and simmer, covered, for 30 minutes. Chill thoroughly before serving. Will keep 1 to 2 months in refrigerator.

Makes 4 to 5 cups

NOTE: To can, pack in hot sterilized jars and seal tightly with vacuum seal lids. Process in hot water bath for 10 minutes, following manufacturer's directions.

RHUBARB CONSERVE ∽

½ cup walnuts	Position **Knife Blade** in **Bowl.** Add nuts; Pulse to chop medium fine. Transfer to small mixing bowl.
6 large stalks rhubarb **Boiling water**	Position **Knife Blade** in **Bowl.** Slice rhubarb. As sliced rhubarb reaches Fill Level, empty into heavy 6-quart pot. Cover rhubarb with boiling water; allow to stand for 3 minutes. Drain; return to 6-quart pot.
1 medium orange, cut in 8 pieces **½ cup raisins**	Position **Knife Blade** in **Bowl;** add orange pieces and raisins. Process to chop, about 15 seconds. Add to rhubarb.
2 cups sugar **¾ cup white vinegar** **¼ teaspoon cinnamon** **⅛ teaspoon ground cloves**	Add sugar, vinegar, cinnamon and cloves to rhubarb. Stir together. Simmer, stirring occasionally, until thick, about 50 minutes.

Stir in nuts. Serve as an accompaniment with poultry, lamb, ham or fish. Will keep several weeks in refrigerator.

Makes about 3½ cups

Ginger-Grapefruit Marmalade and Orange Marmalade

GINGER-GRAPEFRUIT MARMALADE

1 medium white grapefruit	Cut peel on grapefruit into quarter sections; carefully remove without breaking sections. Set grapefruit aside. Cut sections in half crosswise. Pack into bottom of food chute, cut side down. Position **Disc** in **Bowl** with **slicing side up.** Slice peel. Repeat with remaining pieces. Transfer to heavy 8-quart pot.
3 cups water **¼ teaspoon baking soda**	Stir in water and baking soda. Cover and simmer for 20 minutes. Drain and return peel to 8-quart pot.
2 medium white grapefruits **1 medium lemon**	Peel grapefruits and lemon. Discard peel. Break grapefruits (all 3 of them) into sections. Remove seeds and excess membrane. Quarter and seed lemon. Position **Knife Blade** in **Bowl.** Add 1 cup grapefruit. Process to chop finely. Add to pot. Repeat with remaining fruit.
3 cups water **3 cups sugar** **¼ teaspoon ground ginger**	Add water, sugar and ginger to pot. Stir to mix. Bring to a boil over medium heat. Do not cover pot.

Boil, stirring frequently, until thickened, about 1 hour. Test fruit mixture to see if it is thick enough by adding 1 tablespoon to small custard cup. Place in refrigerator to cool for about 3 minutes, then check. Marmalade should be jelled and clear. Pour into hot sterilized jars. Cover with ⅛-inch hot paraffin.

Makes about 4 cups

ORANGE MARMALADE

3 medium oranges **3 medium lemons**	Peel oranges and lemons, cutting off as little white membrane as possible. Position **Knife Blade** in **Bowl;** add half the peel. Process to chop, about 10 seconds. Transfer to heavy 8-quart pot. Repeat with remaining peel.
1½ cups water **¼ teaspoon baking soda**	Add water and baking soda to pot. Cover and simmer 20 minutes. Remove and discard white membrane from peeled fruit. Quarter fruit and remove seeds. Position **Knife Blade** in **Bowl;** add 1 cup fruit. Process until chopped. Add to saucepan. Repeat with remaining fruit. Cover and simmer 10 minutes. Strain fruit mixture, reserving juice. Measure 3 cups of fruit mixture into same 8-quart pot. (Set fruit juice aside for use in fruit flavored gelatin salad or chill and drink.)
5 cups sugar	Add sugar to pot. Over high heat, bring to a full rolling boil; boil hard for 1 minute, stirring constantly.
3 ounces (½ 6-oz. bottle) liquid fruit pectin	Remove from heat and stir in liquid pectin. Skim off foam with metal spoon.

Stir and skim occasionally for 7 minutes. (This helps to cool mixture and keep fruit from floating.) Pour into hot sterilized jars. Cover with ⅛-inch hot paraffin.

Makes 5 cups

Fresh, Home-Baked
Breads

Freshly baked bread is irresistable and mouth-watering delicious. You'll find recipes in this chapter for yeast breads and quick breads, including muffins and biscuits. There's something suitable to serve from breakfast through dinner.

A word about flour: it differs from one region to another. These recipes have been tested with flour from several different parts of the country. Correct measurement is essential for successful baking. Stir flour in canister lightly, then spoon into nested measuring cups without lips or pouring spouts. Level off cup with the edge of a metal spatula or straight knife.

Use these simple techniques for best results. Before processing, distribute ingredients evenly in the Bowl. If ingredients cling to the sides of the Bowl during processing, stop the Processor; remove the cover and scrape down sides of Bowl. If some ingredients appear unblended after processing, stir them together with a rubber spatula.

1. Whole Wheat Bread, page 125
2. Dinner Rolls, page 126
3. Cinnamon Pull Aparts, page 127
4. Banana Bread, page 128
5. Cinnamon Sticky Rolls, page 127
6. Apple Kuchen, page 129

Basic White Bread

BASIC WHITE BREAD ⌒

3 cups all-purpose . . . . . .Position **Knife Blade** in
flour **Bowl;** add flour, dry milk,
¼ cup instant nonfat butter, sugar and salt. Pro-
dry milk solids cess until mixed, about 5
(optional) seconds.
3 tablespoons soft
butter or margarine,
divided in 4 pieces
2 tablespoons sugar
1½ teaspoons salt

1 package active . . . . . . .In measuring cup add
dry yeast yeast to ¼ cup water. Stir
¼ cup lukewarm water and allow to dissolve, about
(110° to 115°F.) 10 minutes. With Processor
⅔ to 1 cup lukewarm running, add yeast mixture
water (110° to through food chute; then,
115°F.) in a slow steady stream,
add just enough of remain-
ing water to make dough
form a loose ball.

Stop processor immediately. (All the water may not be
needed; add only enough to form a soft dough.) Turn
dough out onto well-floured surface and toss or fold over
9 or 10 times by hand. Shape into ball. Place dough in
greased bowl and rotate to grease surface. Cover; let
rise in warm place until doubled in size, about 1½ hours.
Turn dough out onto well-floured surface. Punch down
and toss until no longer sticky. Form into smooth ball. On
floured surface, cover with bowl and let rest 15 minutes.
To shape into loaf, roll dough out on lightly-floured surface to 14×7-inch rectangle. Roll up tightly starting with
7-inch end, sealing ends and bottom with heels of
hands. Place, seam side down, in well-greased 9×5-
inch loaf pan. Cover and let rise in warm place until
dough has risen 1-inch over sides of pan, about 1 hour.
Bake in preheated 375°F. oven until golden brown, about
35 to 40 minutes. Remove from pan immediately.

Makes 1 (9×5-inch) loaf

VARIATION:

French-Style Loaf: Prepare Basic White Bread or Onion
Dill Bread. After dough has risen once, roll out to form a
14×7-inch rectangle. Roll up tightly, starting with the 14-
inch side. Place diagonally on greased cookie sheet.
Brush with mixture of 1 tablespoon egg and 1 teaspoon
water. (Reserve leftover egg for use in cooking.) Slash
top 5 or 6 times. Cover; let rise until doubled, about 1
hour; bake as directed for Basic White Bread.

CINNAMON-RAISIN SWIRL ⌒

1 recipe Basic White . . . . .After dough has risen once,
Bread (opposite) roll out on a lightly-floured
surface to form a 14×7-
inch rectangle.

2 tablespoons sugar . . . . .Combine sugar and cinna-
2 teaspoons cinnamon mon; sprinkle all but 2 tea-
½ cup raisins spoons over dough. Sprinkle
with raisins. Roll dough up
tightly, starting with the 7-
inch end. Place in greased
9×5-inch loaf pan, seam
side down.

1 tablespoon butter, ...Brush with butter and
melted sprinkle with remaining
sugar mixture. Bake as
directed for Basic White
Bread.

Makes 1 (9×5-inch) loaf

ONION DILL BREAD ⌒

1 recipe Basic White . . . .Prepare Basic White Bread
Bread (opposite) as directed in recipe, add-
1 small onion, ing onion and dill weed
quartered with sugar.
2 teaspoons dill weed
or seed

(Rising times will be doubled with this recipe.)

Makes 1 (9×5-inch) loaf

HOW TO MAKE BASIC WHITE BREAD ↝

Stir flour in canister to fluff. Spoon lightly into measuring cup; level with edge of metal spatula.

Position Knife Blade in Bowl. Add dry ingredients and butter. Process until blended, 5 seconds.

Sprinkle yeast over ¼ cup warm water. Stir and allow to dissolve, about 10 minutes.

Add yeast mixture through food chute with Processor running, then just enough water to form dough.

Stop Processor immediately when dough forms a loose ball. All the water may not be needed.

Turn dough out on floured surface; toss and fold over 9 or 10 times by hand.

Shape into ball and place dough in greased bowl. Cover; let rise in warm place until doubled, about 1½ hours.

Turn dough out on floured surface. Toss a few times. Shape as directed in recipe (page 122).

Let loaf rise until doubled. It should come about 1 inch above top of pan.

SWEET WALNUT RING ~

A delectable coffeecake which is sure to please.

1 package active dry yeast
¼ cup lukewarm water (110° to 115°F.) . . . . . . Position **Knife Blade** in **Bowl**; add yeast and water; stir and allow to stand until yeast is dissolved, about 10 minutes.

⅓ cup milk
2 tablespoons butter
2 tablespoons sugar
½ teaspoon salt . . . . In 1-quart saucepan heat milk, butter, sugar and salt until warm (110° to 115°F.)

1¾ cups all-purpose flour . . . . . Add milk mixture and flour to **Bowl**. Process until mixed, about 10 seconds. Turn dough out onto well-floured surface and toss or fold over 9 or 10 times by hand. Shape into ball. Place in greased bowl and rotate to grease surface. Cover and let rise in warm place until doubled in size, about 1½ hours. Punch down. On floured board, roll out into narrow rectangle, 12-inches long and ¼-inch thick.

2 tablespoons soft butter . . . . . . Spread surface of dough with butter.

2 tablespoons brown sugar
½ cup chopped walnuts (page 45)
1 teaspoon cinnamon . . . Sprinkle with brown sugar, walnuts and cinnamon. Roll up from long side; pinch seam to seal. Cut into 1-inch slices. Place slices in overlapping circle on well-greased cookie sheet. Cover; let rise until doubled in size, about 45 minutes. Bake in preheated 375°F. oven for 20 minutes. Cool; carefully remove from cookie sheet.

Confectioners' sugar or frosting . . . . . . Decorate with confectioners' sugar or frosting before serving, if desired.

Makes 1 (11-inch) ring (about 8 servings)

ANADAMA BREAD ~

An old New England favorite.

¼ cup yellow cornmeal
½ cup water . . . . In 2-quart saucepan combine cornmeal and water; mix thoroughly. Place over high heat and stir until cornmeal thickens.

¼ cup molasses
2 tablespoons butter . . . . . . Remove from heat; stir in molasses and butter. Set aside until mixture cools to 120° to 130°F.

2½ cups all-purpose flour
1 package active dry yeast
¾ teaspoon salt . . . . . Position **Knife Blade** in **Bowl**; add flour, yeast, salt and cooled cornmeal mixture. Pulse to blend, 3 to 5 seconds.

½ cup hot tap water (120° to 130°F.) . . . . . With Processor running add water through food chute in a steady stream until dough forms a loose ball.

Do not process longer than 30 seconds. If ball fails to form stop Processor; remove **Knife Blade.** With floured hands shape dough into a ball; place in greased mixing bowl and rotate to grease surface. Cover and let rise in a warm place until doubled in size, about 1 hour. Punch down and shape into one round loaf. Place in a greased, 2-quart round casserole. Let rise until doubled in size, about ½ hour. Bake in preheated 375°F. oven until loaf sounds hollow when tapped, about 45 minutes.

Makes 1 (6½-inch) round loaf

NEAR EASTERN BREAD ~

Flat round little breads which make great sandwiches or dinner accompaniments.

1 cup all-purpose flour
¾ cup whole wheat flour
1 package active dry yeast
½ teaspoon salt . . . . Position **Knife Blade** in **Bowl**; add flour, whole wheat flour, yeast and salt.

¾ cup hot tap water (120° to 130°F.) . . . . . . Add water and process to mix, about 10 seconds.

Dough should form a ball and hold its shape. Turn dough out onto well-floured surface and toss or fold over 9 or 10 times by hand. Shape into ball; place in lightly-greased mixing bowl, turning to grease all sides. Cover and let rise in warm place until doubled in size, about 1½ hours. Punch down; divide into 6 equal pieces. Roll into balls; flatten on ungreased cookie sheet to make discs about 4-inches in diameter. Bake in preheated 350°F. oven for 25 minutes.

Makes 6 (4-inch round) mini loaves

Sally Lunn Bread

WHOLE WHEAT BREAD ∾

2 cups all-purpose flour	. . . . . . Position **Knife Blade** in
1 cup whole wheat flour	**Bowl.** Add ingredients.
2 tablespoons brown sugar	Process until blended,
2 tablespoons soft butter	about 5 seconds.
1½ teaspoons salt	

1 package active dry yeast	. . . . . . In measuring cup add
¼ cup lukewarm water (110° to 115°F.)	yeast to water. Stir and al-
⅔ to 1 cup lukewarm water (110° to 115°F.)	low to dissolve, about 10 minutes. With Processor running, add yeast mixture through food chute; then add enough water in slow steady stream to make the dough form a loose ball.

Stop Processor immediately. (All the water may not be needed; add only enough to form a soft dough.) Turn dough out onto well-floured surface and toss or fold over 9 or 10 times by hand. Shape into ball. Place dough in greased bowl and rotate to grease surface. Cover; let rise in warm place until doubled in size, about 1½ hours. Turn dough out onto well-floured surface. Punch down and toss until no longer sticky. Form into smooth ball. Cover with bowl and let rest 15 minutes. Shape into loaf, as directed for Basic White Bread (page 122). Place in well-greased 9×5-inch pan. Cover and let rise until doubled in size, about 1 hour. Bake in preheated 375°F. oven for 35 to 40 minutes. Turn out of pan immediately.

Makes 1 (9×5-inch) loaf

SALLY LUNN BREAD ∾

A tasty yeast bread that you don't have to knead; simply stir down.

½ cup milk	. . . . In 1-quart saucepan com-
¼ cup butter	bine milk, butter and vine-
2 teaspoons vinegar	gar; heat until warm, 120° to 130°F. (Butter does not need to be completely melted.) Set aside.

2 cups all-purpose flour	. . . . . . Position **Knife Blade** in
¼ cup packed brown sugar	**Bowl;** add flour, sugar,
1 package active dry yeast	yeast, salt, eggs and milk mixture. Process to mix, 5
1 teaspoon salt	seconds. Scrape down
2 eggs	sides of **Bowl,** Pulse 2 to 3 times, until mixture is well mixed. Batter will be loose.

Turn batter into greased mixing bowl. Cover and let rise in a warm place until almost doubled, about 2 hours. Stir down and turn into a well greased and floured 1½-quart round baking dish. Let rise again until doubled, about 45 minutes. Bake in preheated 350°F. oven until golden brown, about 30 to 35 minutes. Allow to cool for 10 minutes before turning out on rack.

Makes 1 (6½-inch) round loaf

GOLDEN RICH BREAD ☜

3 cups all-purpose flour	Position **Knife Blade** in **Bowl**; add flour, dry milk, butter, sugar and salt. Process to mix, 5 seconds.
¼ cup instant nonfat dry milk solids (optional)	
3 tablespoons soft butter or margarine, divided in 4 pieces	
2 tablespoons sugar	
1 teaspoon salt	
1 package active dry yeast	In measuring cup add yeast to water. Stir and allow to dissolve, about 10 minutes.
¼ cup lukewarm water (110° to 115°F.)	
1 egg, slightly beaten	With Processor running add yeast mixture through food chute, then egg. In a slow, steady stream, add just enough water to make dough form a loose ball.
½ to ¾ cup lukewarm water (110° to 115°F.)	

Stop Processor immediately. (All the water may not be needed; add only enough to form a soft dough.) Turn dough out onto well-floured surface and toss or fold over 9 or 10 times by hand. Shape into ball. Place dough in greased bowl and rotate to grease surface. Cover; let rise in warm place until doubled in size, about 1½ hours. Turn dough out onto well-floured surface. Punch down and toss until no longer sticky. Form into smooth ball. On floured surface, cover with bowl and let rest 15 minutes. Shape loaf as directed in Basic White Bread (page 122). Place in well-greased 9×5-inch pan; cover; and let rise in warm place until dough has risen 1-inch over sides of pan, about 1 hour. Bake in preheated 375°F. oven until golden brown, about 35 to 40 minutes. Turn out of pan immediately.

Makes 1 (9×5-inch) loaf

VARIATION:
Dinner Rolls: After dough has risen once, divide dough into 18 to 24 pieces. Shape into balls. Place 2 inches apart on greased cookie sheets. Cover; let rise until doubled, about 1 hour. Bake in preheated 400°F. oven for 12 to 15 minutes. (Dough may also be shaped into other dinner roll forms. See page 127.)

Golden Rich Bread

CINNAMON PULL APARTS ～

1 recipe Golden Rich Bread (page 126)	After dough has risen once, divide into 24 pieces.
¾ cup brown sugar **½ cup coconut** **2 teaspoons cinnamon**	Combine sugar, coconut and cinnamon.
¼ cup butter or margarine	In 1-quart saucepan melt butter.

Coat dough pieces with butter, then roll in sugar mixture. Place coated dough pieces in well-greased 10-inch Bundt pan or tube pan (with solid bottom). Sprinkle any remaining sugar mixture over top. Cover; let rise again until doubled in size, about 1½ hours. Bake in preheated 350°F. oven for 25 to 30 minutes.

Makes 1 (10-inch) loaf

CINNAMON STICKY ROLLS ～

2 tablespoons butter, melted	Coat bottom of a 13×9-inch baking pan with butter.
½ cup walnuts or pecans	Position **Knife Blade** in **Bowl.** Add nuts and Pulse to chop coarsely. Sprinkle nuts over bottom of pan.
1 recipe Golden Rich Bread (page 126) **¼ cup soft butter** **⅓ cup sugar** **⅓ cup brown sugar** **½ to 1 teaspoon cinnamon**	After dough has risen once, roll out on lightly-floured surface to 20×10-inch rectangle. Brush with butter. Sprinkle with sugars, then cinnamon; roll up, from 20-inch side. Cut into 18 pieces.

Place, cut side down, in pan. Cover. Let rise until doubled. Bake in a preheated 350°F. oven for 20 to 25 minutes. Immediately turn out onto rack covered with wax paper.

Makes 18 (2-inch) rolls

HOW TO SHAPE DINNER ROLLS (See Variation, Golden Rich Bread)

Buns: Divide dough into 18 to 24 pieces. Shape into balls. Place 2 inches apart on greased cookie sheet or in greased muffin cups.

Cloverleafs: Divide dough into 12 pieces, then each in thirds. Shape into balls; butter sides lightly. Place 3 in each greased muffin cup.

Finger Rolls: Divide dough into 20 pieces. Shape in 4-inch strips. Butter sides; place in 2 rows in greased 10×8- or 9×9-inch pan.

Crescents: Divide dough in half. Roll each half on floured surface to 12-inch circle. Brush with melted butter. Cut into 9 wedges. Starting with wide end, roll up wedges. Place, point side down, on greased cookie sheet; curve slightly.

Pinwheels: Roll out dough on floured surface to 20×10-inch rectangle. Brush with soft butter. Roll up from 20-inch side. Cut into 24 pieces. Place, cut side down, in greased muffin cups or 12×9-inch pan.

Four-Leaf Clovers: Divide dough into 12 pieces; shape into balls. Place in greased muffin cups. With greased scissors, cut each in half almost to bottom, then in quarters.

SUNNY DATE 'N NUT BREAD

1 cup chopped, pitted dates	Combine dates, water and baking soda in small mixing bowl; set aside. Grease and flour a 9×5-inch loaf pan. Preheat oven to 350°F.
¾ cup boiling water	
1 teaspoon baking soda	
1 small orange, cut in 6 pieces, seeded	Position **Knife Blade** in **Bowl.** Add orange pieces; process to chop, about 15 seconds. Add flour, nuts, sugar, eggs, butter, salt and half the date mixture. Process to mix, 5 seconds. Add remaining date mixture; process until well mixed, about 15 to 20 seconds. Pour into loaf pan. Bake until loaf springs back when touched lightly in center, 55 to 65 minutes. Cool 10 minutes. Loosen sides with spatula and remove from pan.
1½ cups all-purpose flour	
1 cup nuts (optional)	
¾ cup sugar	
2 eggs	
2 tablespoons butter or margarine, cut in 4 pieces	
1 teaspoon salt	

Makes 1 (9×5-inch) loaf

GARDEN FRESH ZUCCHINI BREAD

1 cup walnuts	Preheat oven to 350°F. Position **Disc** in **Bowl** with **slicing side up.** Slice walnuts. Set aside.
1 medium zucchini, cut to fit food chute	Position **Disc** in **Bowl** with **shredding side up.** Shred zucchini. (You should have about 1½ cups.) Set aside.
½ cup vegetable oil	Position **Knife Blade** in **Bowl.** Add oil, sugar, eggs, vanilla, baking soda, cinnamon, salt and baking powder. Process to mix, about 15 seconds.
1 cup sugar	
2 eggs	
2 teaspoons vanilla	
½ teaspoon baking soda	
½ teaspoon cinnamon	
½ teaspoon salt	
¼ teaspoon baking powder	
1½ cups all-purpose flour	Add flour to **Bowl.** Pulse 2 or 3 times to mix. Stop and scrape down sides of **Bowl.** Pulse 1 or 2 times more.

Remove **Knife Blade.** Add nuts and zucchini; stir in by hand. Pour batter into greased and floured 9×5-inch loaf pan. Bake until loaf tests done, about 1¼ hours.

Makes 1 (9×5-inch) loaf

BANANA BREAD

2 very ripe medium bananas, peeled, cut in 1-inch pieces	Preheat oven to 350°F. Position **Knife Blade** in **Bowl.** Add bananas and butter; process until finely chopped, about 20 seconds.
½ cup butter or margarine, chilled, cut in 6 pieces	
1½ cups all-purpose flour	Add remaining ingredients; process 10 seconds. Turn off.
¾ cup sugar	
2 eggs	
¼ cup milk	
2 teaspoons lemon juice or vinegar	
1 teaspoon baking soda	
½ teaspoon salt	
½ cup walnuts or pecans (optional)	Scrape down sides of **Bowl** with rubber spatula. Add nuts, if desired. Process 2 to 3 seconds longer.

Do not overprocess, this will make bread coarse. Turn into greased 9×5-inch loaf pan. Bake until bread springs back when touched lightly in center, about 55 to 60 minutes. Cool before removing from pan.

Makes 1 (9×5-inch) loaf

Sunny Date 'N Nut Bread

Apple Kuchen

APPLE KUCHEN ⌒ ◐

A moist coffeecake, good in the morning or as a dessert.

Streusel Topping:

½ **cup all-purpose flour**	Preheat oven to 350°F. Position **Knife Blade** in **Bowl**; add flour, sugar, butter and cinnamon. Process until crumbly, about 20 seconds. Transfer to large mixing bowl.
⅓ **cup sugar**	
3 **tablespoons butter or margarine, chilled, cut in 3 pieces**	
¼ **teaspoon cinnamon or nutmeg**	
2 **medium apples, peeled, quartered, cored**	Position **Disc** in **Bowl** with **slicing side up;** slice apples. Add to Streusel and stir to coat apple slices.

Cake:

1½ **cups all-purpose flour**	Position **Knife Blade** in **Bowl.** Add flour, sugar and butter; process until butter is cut into flour and sugar, about 15 seconds. Add remaining ingredients. Process 5 seconds. Turn off. Scrape down sides of **Bowl.** Process 5 seconds longer. Spread batter in greased 9×9-inch baking pan.
¾ **cup sugar**	
¼ **cup butter or margarine, chilled, cut in 3 pieces**	
½ **cup milk**	
2 **eggs**	
2 **teaspoons baking powder**	
1 **teaspoon salt**	
1 **teaspoon vanilla**	

Neatly arrange apple/streusel mixture on top. Bake until cake is set and apples are tender, about 40 to 45 minutes. If used as dessert, top with whipped cream, if desired.

Makes 1 (9×9-inch) coffeecake

VARIATION:
Cranberry Kuchen: Substitute 1½ cups fresh or frozen and thawed cranberries for apples. Pulse, using **Knife Blade,** to chop coarsely, about 10 seconds.

BASIC BLENDER CREPES ▽

1½ **cups milk**	Add all ingredients to **Blender Jar.** Cover and process at Stir speed until blended, 20 to 25 seconds. Scrape down flour on sides of **Jar;** process 5 seconds more.
3 **eggs**	
1¾ **cups all-purpose flour**	
2 **tablespoons butter or margarine, melted**	

Heat a 7-inch, lightly-greased skillet over medium high heat until water drop dances when sprinkled on it. (Or use electric crepe maker.) Pour 2 tablespoons batter at a time into skillet. Quickly tilt skillet to cover bottom. Pour off extra batter into **Blender Jar.** Brown on first side, about ½ minute; turn to brown on second side. Stack with wax paper between every 4 crepes. Place in plastic bag until ready to fill.*

Makes 16 to 18 (7-inch) crepes

*Crepes can be made ahead and refrigerated or frozen.

VARIATION:
Dessert Crepes: Add 2 tablespoons confectioners' sugar. If desired, also add 1 to 2 tablespoons rum, brandy or fruit flavored liqueur.

SPEEDY BLENDER WAFFLES ▽

¾ **cup milk**	Add all ingredients to **Blender Jar.** Cover and blend at Stir speed for 10 seconds. Turn off. Scrape down sides of **Jar** and blend at Stir speed 5 seconds longer. Bake in waffle baker according to manufacturer's directions.
2 **eggs**	
2 **tablespoons vegetable oil**	
1 **cup all-purpose flour**	
1½ **teaspoons baking powder**	
1½ **teaspoons sugar**	
½ **teaspoon salt**	

Makes 2 cups batter
(about 2 4-section waffles)

Lightening Biscuits with Orange Marmalade (page 119)

LIGHTENING BISCUITS ∾

2 cups all-purpose flour	Preheat oven to 450°F. Position **Knife Blade** in **Bowl**; add flour, baking powder, salt and butter. Process until particles are fine, about 15 seconds.
1 tablespoon baking powder	
½ teaspoon salt	
¼ cup butter or margarine, chilled, cut in 3 pieces	
⅔ cup milk	With Processor running add milk, all at once, through food chute.

Process until dough forms into a ball, about 7 seconds. Dough will be slightly sticky. Knead 10 times on floured surface. Pat or roll out to ½-inch thickness for high biscuits, ¼-inch for thin crusty biscuits. Cut into rounds with 2-inch floured cutter or glass of the same size. Place close together on ungreased cookie sheet and bake until golden brown, 10 to 12 minutes. Serve hot.

Makes 12 high or 24 thin crusty biscuits

VARIATIONS:
Cheese Biscuits: Before mixing biscuits, shred 4 ounces natural Cheddar or Parmesan cheese. Reserve in small mixing bowl. Add to mixture just before milk.

READY-TO-GO BISCUIT MIX ∾

If you serve biscuits frequently, keep this mix on hand.

3 cups all-purpose flour	Position **Knife Blade** in **Bowl**. Add flour, baking powder and salt. Distribute shortening over dry ingredients. Process until well mixed, about 10 seconds.
2 tablespoons baking powder*	
1 teaspoon salt*	
⅓ cup shortening, divided in 3 pieces	

Store in tightly covered container in refrigerator. Keeps up to 4 weeks.

Makes 3¾ cups

*If self-rising flour is used, omit baking powder and salt.

To Use:

1 cup Ready-To-Go Biscuit Mix	Preheat oven to 450°F. Position **Knife Blade** in **Bowl**. Add Ready-To-Go Biscuit Mix.
¼ to ⅓ cup milk	With Processor running add just enough milk through food chute to form dough, about 3 to 4 seconds. (All milk may not be needed.)

Dough should be soft and slightly sticky. Toss or fold dough over on floured surface, about 10 times. Roll out to ¼- or ½-inch thickness. Cut into rounds with floured 2-inch cookie cutter. Place on ungreased cookie sheet. Bake 12 to 15 minutes.

Makes 8 to 10 thin biscuits or 4 to 5 high biscuits

TEA BISCUITS ∾

2¼ cups all-purpose flour	Preheat oven to 425°F. Position **Knife Blade** in **Bowl**; add flour, baking powder, sugar, salt and butter. Process until butter is evenly cut into flour mixture, about 15 seconds.
1 tablespoon baking powder	
1 tablespoon sugar	
¼ teaspoon salt	
¼ cup butter or margarine, chilled, cut in 4 pieces	
½ cup milk	Whisk milk and egg together. With Processor running add milk mixture, all at once, through food chute. Process until well mixed, about 10 seconds.
1 egg	

Transfer dough to lightly floured board. Pat dough into a 7-inch square about ½-inch thick. Cut into 12 portions. Place on greased cookie sheet. Bake until golden brown, about 12 to 15 minutes. Serve hot with butter and jam.

Makes 1 dozen (2-inch) biscuits

OATMEAL BISCUITS ❧

1 cup all-purpose flour . . . .Preheat oven to
1 tablespoon baking
    powder
½ teaspoon salt
2 tablespoons butter,
    chilled, cut in
    3 pieces

1 cup quick oats, ...Ac
    uncooked   to
1 egg, slightly beaten   mo
⅓ cup milk   (If
2 tablespoons honey   mix
                              spa

Drop by well-rounded tablespo
cookie sheet. Bake 8 to 10 minute

                              Make

RAISIN BRAN MUFFINS ❧

n flakes . . . . . .Preheat oven to 400°F. Po-
                    sition **Knife Blade** in **Bowl.**
s   Add bran flakes, milk and
                    raisins; let stand 10 min-
                    utes.

rpose . . . . .Add remaining ingredients
                    to **Bowl.** Process just until
ses   mixed, about 4 to 5 Pulses.
                    Fill well-greased muffin
le oil   cups ⅔ full. Bake until muf-
                    fins spring back when
baking   touched lightly in center,
                    about 20 to 22 minutes.
t   Loosen muffins with spat-
                    ula. Serve warm.

Makes 1 dozen (2½-inch) muffins

nuffins, wrap in foil and heat at 350°F.
oast-R-Oven® Toaster for 10 minutes.

Oatmeal Biscuits, Raisin Bran Muffins

Everybody's Favorite
Desserts

"What's for dessert?" Here you'll find a variety of answers for any occasion: family favorites, dramatic desserts, traditional holiday specialties.

If you're making cake, cookies or pie, follow the flour measuring directions on page 123. The pie fillings in this cookbook were created for a standard 1¼-inch deep pie shell — the kind you'll make with speed and ease using a Food Processor. Take pride in your pastry, but don't forget the different desserts processing makes possible.

Butter Cake Loaf, Toasted Butter Pecan Loaf, Cherry Loaf

Cakes

HONEY TEA CAKE 🍮〰️

2 cups pecans or walnuts	Preheat oven to 300°F. Position **Disc** in **Bowl** with **slicing side up;** slice nuts. Transfer to large mixing bowl.
2 jars (3½-oz. each) candied cherries, red or green **2 cups all-purpose flour** **1 cup all-purpose flour**	Position **Knife Blade** in **Bowl;** add cherries and 2 cups flour. Process until cherries are coarsely chopped, about 3 seconds. Add to chopped nuts with remaining 1 cup flour.
1 cup butter, chilled, cut in 1-inch pieces **1 cup honey** **4 eggs** **¼ cup bourbon or orange juice**	Position **Knife Blade** in **Bowl;** combine remaining ingredients. Process until butter is evenly cut into mixture, about 20 to 30 seconds.

Pour over dry, chopped ingredients; mix well by hand. Pour into ungreased 10-inch tube pan. Bake until golden brown, 1 hour and 20 minutes. (Cake will be low.) Cool completely. Remove from pan and sprinkle top with confectioners' sugar, if desired.

Makes 1 (10-inch) cake

UPSIDE DOWN APPLE CAKE 🍮〰️

¼ cup butter or margarine, melted **½ cup pecans or walnuts** **½ cup packed brown sugar** **½ teaspoon cinnamon**	Preheat oven to 350°F. Add butter to bottom of 9-inch round cake pan*. Sprinkle with pecans, brown sugar and cinnamon.
3 medium apples, peeled, quartered, cored	Position **Disc** in **Bowl** with **slicing side up.** Slice apples. Place in bottom of pan.
1 cup all-purpose flour **⅔ cup sugar** **½ cup milk** **¼ cup shortening, divided in 4 pieces** **1 egg** **1½ teaspoons baking powder** **½ teaspoon salt** **½ teaspoon vanilla**	Position **Knife Blade** in **Bowl.** Add remaining ingredients. Process until well mixed and creamy, 25 to 30 seconds. Spoon over apples and spread evenly. Bake until cake springs back when touched lightly in center, 40 to 45 minutes. Loosen sides of cake and turn out on large serving plate.

Serve warm or cold. Top with whipped cream or ice cream, if desired.

Makes 1 (9-inch) cake
(about 6 to 8 servings)

*A 9-inch deep-dish pie pan or 10-inch pie pan may be used.

BUTTER CAKE LOAF 👁

1 cup sugar	Preheat oven to 350°F.
½ cup soft butter or margarine, cut in 10 pieces	Grease and flour a 9×5-inch loaf pan. Position **Knife Blade** in **Bowl**; add all ingredients except flour. Process 30 seconds. Stir down sides of **Bowl**.
½ cup milk	
2 eggs	
1½ teaspoons baking powder	
1 teaspoon vanilla	
½ teaspoon salt	
1½ cups all-purpose flour	Add flour to processed mixture. Process to mix in flour, about 5 seconds.

Pour into loaf pan. Bake until cake springs back when lightly touched in center, about 50 to 60 minutes. Cool 20 minutes and remove from pan.

Makes 1 (9×5-inch) cake

VARIATIONS:

Cherry Loaf: Omit vanilla from Butter Cake Loaf. Add ⅓ cup well-drained maraschino cherries and ½ teaspoon almond extract to butter and sugar mixture before processing.

Ambrosia Cake: Omit vanilla from Butter Cake Loaf and substitute ½ teaspoon lemon extract. Add ½ cup coconut to butter and sugar mixture before processing.

Swedish Nut Cake: Omit vanilla from Butter Cake Loaf and substitute ½ teaspoon almond extract. Add ⅔ cup filberts to butter and sugar mixture before processing.

Toasted Butter Pecan Loaf: Melt 3 tablespoons butter in 1-quart saucepan over medium low heat; add ½ cup pecans. Brown butter and pecans, stirring constantly. With slotted spoon remove pecans from butter, and add to butter and sugar mixture before processing. Set butter aside. When baked cake is cool, stir 1 cup confectioners' sugar into browned butter. Add 2 to 3 teaspoons milk to make a smooth frosting. Spread on cake.

BLUEBERRY BUCKLE 👁

Cake:

2 cups blueberries, fresh or frozen and thawed	Wash and drain blueberries. Set aside on paper towels to dry.
1 teaspoon lemon juice	Stir lemon juice into milk; set aside. Preheat oven to 350°F.
⅓ cup milk	
¼ cup butter, chilled, cut in 4 pieces	Position **Knife Blade** in **Bowl**. Add butter, sugar, egg and lemon rind. Process to chop rind and mix ingredients, about 20 seconds. Pour milk mixture through food chute with Processor running. Turn off.
¾ cup sugar	
1 egg	
4 1-inch square pieces lemon rind	
1½ cups all-purpose flour	Add flour, baking powder and salt. Pulse quickly 3 or 4 times to mix ingredients. Do not overprocess. Remove **Knife Blade** from **Bowl**. Add blueberries. Gently stir by hand to mix. Spread batter in greased 8-inch square baking pan. Bake until cake tests done, 40 to 45 minutes.
2 teaspoons baking powder	
½ teaspoon salt	

Glaze:

2 tablespoons soft butter	Just before cake is done, combine butter, sugar and lemon juice. Cook over low heat until smooth. Remove from heat.
¼ cup sugar	
1 tablespoon lemon juice	

When cake is done, spread glaze over top. Return to oven. Broil until glaze bubbles. Watch to avoid over-browning.

Makes 16 (1½-inch) squares

Blueberry Buckle

Aloha Carrot Cake

ALOHA CARROT CAKE ✍ 🍥

3 medium carrots, peeled	Preheat oven to 375°F. Position **Knife Blade** in **Bowl** with **Disc** above it, **shredding side up.** Shred carrots. Add carrot pieces remaining on **Disc** and process 5 seconds longer.
1 cup sugar **½ cup vegetable oil** **2 eggs** **1 teaspoon baking powder** **1 teaspoon baking soda** **1 teaspoon cinnamon** **1 teaspoon salt** **¼ teaspoon mace**	Add sugar, oil, eggs, baking powder and soda, cinnamon, salt and mace. Process to mix, 30 seconds.
1½ cups all-purpose flour **1 can (8¼-oz.) crushed pineapple, undrained**	Add flour. Process to combine, 15 seconds. Add pineapple; Pulse until just mixed, about 2 to 3 seconds.

Turn into a greased and floured 9-inch square baking pan. Bake until cake springs back when lightly touched in center, 30 to 35 minutes. Cool and remove from pan, if desired. Frost with Cream Cheese Frosting. Refrigerate any unused portion.

Makes 1 (9-inch square) cake

CREAM CHEESE FROSTING ✍

1 package (3-oz.) cream cheese, chilled, cut in 4 pieces **2 tablespoons soft butter or margarine** **2 to 3 teaspoons lemon juice**	Position **Knife Blade** in **Bowl.** Drop cream cheese through food chute, one piece at a time, with Processor running. Turn off. Add butter and lemon juice. Process to mix ingredients, 3 to 4 seconds.
1½ cups confectioners' sugar **¼ teaspoon mace**	Add sugar and mace. Process until smooth, 15 to 20 seconds.

Makes 1 cup

ORANGE RAISIN CAKE ✍ 🍥

Cake:

1 cup sugar **¾ cup raisins** **⅓ cup shortening, divided in 4 pieces** **2 eggs** **1 teaspoon salt** **1 teaspoon baking soda**	Preheat oven to 350°F. Position **Knife Blade** in **Bowl**; add sugar, raisins, shortening, eggs, salt and baking soda.
1 small orange, cut in half	Position **Knife Blade** in **Bowl** with **Disc** above it, **slicing side up**; slice orange. Remove **Disc**; add any remaining peel to **Bowl**. Process until well mixed and raisins are fine, 1 to 1½ minutes.
1½ cups all-purpose flour **½ cup milk** **½ cup nuts**	Add flour, milk and nuts; process just until mixed, 3 to 4 seconds. Spread in greased and floured 9-inch square baking pan. Bake until cake springs back when touched lightly in center, 35 to 40 minutes. Cool. Leave in pan and frost.

Orange Frosting:

1½ cups confectioners' sugar **2 tablespoons soft butter or margarine** **4 1-inch square pieces orange rind**	Position **Knife Blade** in **Bowl**; add sugar, butter and orange rind. Process to chop rind, about 20 seconds.
1 tablespoon lemon juice **2 teaspoons water**	Add lemon juice and water through food chute with Processor running.

Process until smooth and spreadable. Add a few more drops water if needed.

Makes 1 (9×9-inch) frosted cake

Pies & Pastries

RED APPLE BERRY PIE ✌ ◗

1 recipe two crust pie crust (pages 138 & 139)	Roll out half the doug[h on] a well floured surface [and] fit into a 9-inch pie pan. [Pre]heat oven to 450°F.
2 cups fresh or frozen and thawed cranberries	Position **Knife Blade** [in] **Bowl;** chop cranberrie[s] coarsely, 4 to 5 seconds. Place in large mixing bowl.
4 medium cooking apples, peeled, cored, quartered	Position **Disc** in **Bowl** with **slicing side up;** slice apples; add to cranberries.
1½ cups sugar* **2 tablespoons all-purpose flour** **¼ teaspoon nutmeg**	Add sugar, flour and nutmeg to fruit. Stir well to mix. Fill pie crust. Roll out remaining dough and place over fruit.

Fold top edge under bottom crust; press to seal. Flute edge (page 138) and cut slits in center. Bake for 10 minutes; reduce heat to 375°F. Bake until apples are tender and crust is well browned, 35 to 40 minutes longer.

Makes 1 (9-inch) pie

*For a tangy, tart filling, decrease sugar to 1 cup.

PUMPKIN PIE ✌

1 unbaked 9-inch pie crust (pages 138 & 139)	Prepare pie crust with high fluted edge (page 138).
1 can (30-oz.) pumpkin pie mix **2 eggs** **1 small can (⅔ cup) evaporated milk**	Position **Knife Blade** in **Bowl.** Combine pumpkin pie mix, eggs and milk in **Bowl.** Process until smooth, about 15 seconds. Pour into pie crust.
½ teaspoon nutmeg (optional)	Sprinkle top of pie with nutmeg, if desired.

Follow directions on pumpkin pie mix for baking time and temperature.

Makes 1 (9-inch) pie

Red Apple Berry Pie

How to Flute Pie Crust

HOW TO FLUTE PIE CRUST

Trim pastry so it extends ½- to ¾-inch beyond rim of pan. Turn under to form a doubled edge. Hold the forefinger of one hand against rim of crust and squeeze pastry against it with thumb and forefinger of other hand.

ONE CRUST LARD PIE CRUST ✍

1 cup all-purpose flour	Follow directions for One Crust Butter Pie Crust (opposite). If crust is to be baked before filling, prick with fork and bake in pre-heated 450°F. oven for 12 to 15 minutes.
¼ cup lard, chilled, cut in thirds	
½ teaspoon salt	
3 tablespoons cold water	

Makes 1 (9-inch) pie crust

TWO CRUST LARD PIE CRUST ✍

2¼ cups all-purpose flour	Follow directions for One Crust Butter Pie Crust (opposite), adding the extra tablespoon water only if dough does not hold to-gether. Divide in half and shape into 2 balls.
1 teaspoon salt	
½ cup lard, chilled, cut in 6 pieces	
⅓ cup cold water and 1 tablespoon cold water	

Makes 2 (9-inch) pie crusts or 1 double crust pie

ONE CRUST BUTTER PIE CRUST ✍

1 cup all-purpose flour	Position **Knife Blade** in **Bowl;** add flour, salt and butter. Process until parti-cles resemble coarse crumbs, about 15 seconds.
¼ teaspoon salt	
¼ cup butter or margarine, frozen, cut in thirds	
3 tablespoons cold water	Add water all at once through food chute with Processor running.

Process until dough forms a ball, or no more than 20 to 30 seconds. If dough does not form a ball, stop Processor. Remove **Knife Blade.** Shape into ball with hands. Chill ½ hour, if necessary, for easier handling. Roll out for pie, or as directed in recipe. If crust is to be baked before filling, prick generously with fork. Bake in preheated 475°F. oven until golden brown, 12 to 15 minutes.

Makes 1 (9-inch) pie crust

GRAHAM CRACKER PIE CRUST ✍ ⚫

22 2½-inch graham cracker squares* (about 1⅓ cups)	Position **Knife Blade** in **Bowl** with **Disc** above it, **shredding side up.** Crumb crackers following direc-tions for crumbing dry bread (page 21).
5 tablespoons soft butter or margarine	Remove cover and **Disc.** Add butter and sugar; Pulse to mix, 2 to 3 seconds.
2 tablespoons sugar	

Preheat oven to 375°F. Set aside ¼ cup crumbs for sprinkling on top of pie filling. Press remainder firmly into 9-inch pie pan. Bake for 6 to 8 minutes. Cool before filling.

Makes 1 (9-inch) pie crust

*If using 8-inch pie pan, use 18 crackers (about 1 cup crumbs) and 4 tablespoons soft butter or margarine.

VARIATIONS:
For a crunchier toasted flavor, melt butter in 12-inch skil-let and carefully brown crumbs in butter over high heat for 1 to 2 minutes. Then press into pie pan and chill. No need to bake.

Substitute 1⅓ cups of any of the following crumbs: gin-ger snaps, vanilla wafers, rice cereal. Omit sugar when using cookies.

TWO CRUST BUTTER PIE CRUST ✍

2 cups all-purpose flour	Follow directions for One Crust Butter Pie Crust (above), but divide dough in half and shape into 2 balls.
1 teaspoon salt	
½ cup butter, frozen, cut in 6 pieces	
⅓ cup cold water	

Makes 2 (9-inch) pie crusts or 1 double crust pie

ONE CRUST STANDARD PIE CRUST ∾

1 cup all-purpose . . . .
flour
½ teaspoon salt
¼ cup vegetable
shortening, room
temperature, divided
in 3 pieces
1 tablespoon butter or
margarine, frozen
3 tablespoons cold
water

Follow directions for One Crust Butter Pie Crust (page 138). If crust is to be baked before filling, prick generously with fork and bake in preheated 450°F. oven for 9 to 12 minutes.

Makes 1 (9-inch) pie crust

TWO CRUST STANDARD PIE CRUST ∾

2 cups all-purpose . . . .
flour
1 teaspoon salt
½ cup vegetable
shortening, room
temperature, divided
in 6 pieces
1 tablespoon butter or
margarine, frozen
⅓ cup cold water

Follow directions for One Crust Butter Pie Crust (page 138), but divide dough in half and shape into 2 balls.

Makes 2 (9-inch) pie crusts
or 1 double crust pie

HOW TO MAKE PIE DOUGH ∾

Stir flour in canister 2 or 3 times to fluff up. Spoon lightly into dry nested type measuring cup. Level with straight edge of metal spatula or knife.

Position Knife Blade in Bowl. Add flour and salt, then pieces of lard, shortening or frozen butter.

Process until particles resemble coarse crumbs, about 20 seconds.

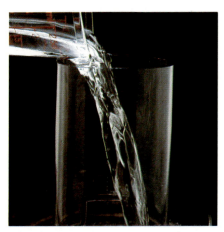

Add cold water, all at once through food chute with Processor running.

Process no more than 20 to 30 seconds. If dough forms a ball before that time, stop Processor.

Stop processing after 30 seconds. Longer processing toughens dough. Dough will not always form a ball. If not, shape into ball by hand.

Apple and Cream Pie

APPLE AND CREAM PIE 🐦🐦

¾ cup walnuts	Position **Knife Blade** in **Bowl**. Add walnuts. Pulse to chop coarsely. Set aside in small mixing bowl.
4 medium cooking apples, peeled, cored, quartered	Preheat oven to 450°F. Position **Disc** in **Bowl** with **slicing side up**. Slice apples (page 19). Transfer slices to pie crust.
1 unbaked 9-inch pie crust (pages 138 & 139)	
1 cup whipping cream . . . **1 cup sugar** **1 egg** **3 tablespoons all-purpose flour** **1 teaspoon cinnamon** **1 teaspoon vanilla** **¼ teaspoon nutmeg** **⅛ teaspoon salt**	Position **Knife Blade** in **Bowl**. Add cream, sugar, egg, flour and seasonings. Process to mix thoroughly, about 10 seconds. Pour over apple slices. Sprinkle top with walnuts.

Bake for 10 minutes at 450°F.; reduce heat to 350°F. Bake until apples are tender, 35 to 40 minutes longer.

Makes 1 (9-inch) pie

COCONUT CUSTARD PIE 🥛

1 unbaked 9-inch pie crust with high fluted edge (pages 138 & 139)	Prepare pie crust. Preheat oven to 375°F. Place a piece of aluminum foil over pie crust in pan and fill with dry beans to weigh down pastry and prevent it from puffing as it bakes. Bake for 20 minutes. Remove foil and beans.
2 cups warm milk . . . . **4 eggs** **½ cup sugar** **½ teaspoon salt**	Place milk, eggs, sugar and salt in **Blender Jar**. Cover; blend at Stir speed for 5 seconds.
1 can (3½-oz.) shredded coconut (about 1⅓ cups) **Nutmeg**	Sprinkle coconut over pie crust. Pour milk mixture over coconut. Sprinkle surface with nutmeg.

Bake until knife inserted 3 inches from edge comes out clean, about 30 to 35 minutes. (Center may appear soft but will set later.) Cool before serving. Refrigerate leftover pie.

Makes 1 (9-inch) pie

Cookies

CHEESECAKE BARS 👁 🌑

26 2½-inch graham cracker squares, broken in quarters (1½ cups crumbs)	Preheat oven to 350°F. Position **Knife Blade** in **Bowl** with **Disc** above it, **shredding side up.** Crumb graham crackers.
1 package (6-oz.) butterscotch chips 5 tablespoons butter	In 1-quart saucepan, combine butterscotch chips and butter and melt over low heat. Remove from heat. Stir in crumbs. Set aside ½ cup of mixture. Press remaining mixture into ungreased 8-inch square baking pan. Bake 10 minutes.
1 package (8-oz.) cream cheese, chilled, cut in 6 pieces ¼ cup sugar 2 eggs 2 tablespoons all-purpose flour 1 tablespoon lemon juice	Position **Knife Blade** in **Bowl;** add remaining ingredients. Process until smooth, about 10 seconds. Spread over hot, baked crust. Sprinkle reserved crumb mixture over top. Return to oven and bake 20 to 25 minutes. Cool and cut into squares. Store in refrigerator.

Makes 16 (2-inch) squares

CHEWY FRUIT SQUARES 👁

¾ cup walnuts	Preheat oven to 325°F. Position **Knife Blade** in **Bowl.** Add walnuts. Pulse to chop coarsely. Set aside.
1½ cups all-purpose flour ¼ cup packed brown sugar ½ cup butter, chilled, cut in 6 pieces	Position **Knife Blade** in **Bowl;** add flour, brown sugar and butter. Process until butter is thoroughly cut into dry ingredients, about 20 seconds.
1 egg, slightly beaten 1 cup raisins	Distribute slightly beaten egg, raisins and reserved nuts over mixture in **Bowl.**

Process until mixture clings together, about 15 to 20 seconds. Using spatula, spread evenly over greased 9-inch square pan. Press dough down along edges. Bake 25 to 30 minutes. Cut into squares immediately.

Makes 16 (2-inch) squares

Top to bottom: Heavenly Almond Bars, Chocolate In-Betweens, Cheesecake Bars, Chewy Fruit Squares, Sweet Dream Bars

CHOCOLATE IN-BETWEENS ❧

1 cup packed brown sugar **¾ cup butter or margarine, chilled, cut in 8 pieces** **½ teaspoon salt**	Preheat oven to 350°F. Position **Knife Blade** in **Bowl;** add brown sugar, butter and salt. Process to mix, about 15 seconds. Mixture will be lumpy. Stop if mixture begins to form a ball.
1½ cups all-purpose flour **1 cup quick oats, uncooked**	Add flour and oats to mixture. Pulse to crumble, 2 to 3 times. Stir down mixture. Repeat Pulsing until mixture is crumbly. Press about ⅔ mixture (2½ cups) into bottom of greased 13×9-inch baking pan. Leave remaining ⅓ mixture in **Bowl.**
1 can (14-oz.) sweetened condensed milk **1 package (6-oz.) semi-sweet chocolate chips**	In 2-quart saucepan, combine condensed milk and chips. Heat over low heat, stirring constantly, until chips melt. (Be careful; do not let chocolate burn.)

Pour over crust in pan. Sprinkle remaining crumbs over top. Bake until lightly browned, 25 to 30 minutes.

Makes 2 dozen (2-inch) squares

HEAVENLY ALMOND BARS ❧

8 ounces blanched almonds	Preheat oven to 350°F. Position **Knife Blade** in **Bowl.** Add almonds. Process until finely ground, about 20 seconds. Set aside in small mixing bowl.
½ cup soft butter or margarine **⅓ cup sugar** **3 egg yolks** **2 teaspoons baking powder** **⅛ teaspoon salt**	Position **Knife Blade** in **Bowl.** Add butter, sugar, egg yolks, baking powder and salt. Process to mix, about 15 seconds.
1½ cups all-purpose flour	Add flour. Pulse to mix, about 5 to 6 Pulses. Spread and pat into ungreased 9-inch square baking pan.
3 egg whites **½ cup sugar** **1 teaspoon almond extract**	With mixer, beat egg whites in large mixing bowl until stiff, but not dry. Gradually add sugar and almond extract. Fold almonds in by hand.

Stir to thoroughly mix. Pour mixture over bottom layer. Bake 25 to 30 minutes. Cut into bars while warm.

Makes 32 (2×1-inch) bars

SWEET DREAM BARS ❧

½ cup soft butter or margarine, cut in 6 pieces **½ cup packed brown sugar**	Preheat oven to 350°F. Position **Knife Blade** in **Bowl;** add butter and sugar. Pulse to mix, about 10 seconds. Scrape down sides of **Bowl** and process 10 seconds longer.
1½ cups all-purpose flour	Add flour to **Bowl;** Pulse until mixture resembles coarse crumbs, 10 to 15 seconds. Press firmly into bottom of ungreased 13×9-inch baking pan. Bake 15 minutes.
3 eggs	Position **Knife Blade** in **Bowl;** add eggs. Process until foamy, about 5 seconds.
1 cup packed brown sugar **1 cup flaked or fresh shredded coconut (page 26)** **2 tablespoons all-purpose flour** **1 teaspoon baking powder** **1 teaspoon vanilla** **¼ teaspoon salt**	Add remaining ingredients. Process until well mixed and foamy, about 10 seconds. Pour over partially baked crust. Bake until golden brown, 18 to 20 minutes. Sprinkle with confectioners' sugar, if desired. Cool and cut into squares.

Makes 2 dozen (2-inch) squares

PECAN BALLS ❧

1½ cups pecan halves	Preheat oven to 300°F. Position **Knife Blade** in **Bowl;** add pecans. Process until finely chopped, about 5 seconds. Transfer to large mixing bowl.
2 cups all-purpose flour **1 cup butter or margarine, chilled, cut in 1-inch pieces** **¼ cup packed brown sugar** **1 tablespoon water** **2 teaspoons vanilla**	Position **Knife Blade** in **Bowl;** add remaining ingredients. Process until dough is mixed and sticks together, about 30 seconds. Add to pecans and mix together with hands. Form into small, ¾-inch balls. Place on ungreased cookie sheets; bake 30 to 35 minutes. Sprinkle with confectioners' sugar while hot, if desired.

Makes 5 dozen cookies

PEANUT CHIPS ✎

½ cup soft butter or . . . . .Preheat oven to 350°F. Po-
margarine   sition **Knife Blade** in **Bowl;**
½ cup packed brown   add butter, sugar, egg,
sugar   vanilla and cinnamon. Pro-
1 egg   cess until smooth and
1 teaspoon vanilla   creamy, about 10 seconds.
½ teaspoon cinnamon

1¼ cups all-purpose . . . . .Add flour and peanuts. Pro-
flour   cess until flour is just mixed
1 cup salted peanuts   in, about 10 seconds.

Spread out to form a 14×10-inch rectangle on a large
greased cookie sheet. Bake until light golden brown,
about 12 to 15 minutes. Immediately cut into 2-inch
squares and remove from cookie sheet.

Makes 35 (2-inch) chips

REAL PEANUT-BUTTER COOKIES ✎

1 cup salted peanuts . . .Preheat oven to 350°F. Position **Knife Blade** in **Bowl;**
add peanuts. Process to a
chunky peanut butter stage,
about 2 minutes.

1 cup packed brown . . . .Add brown sugar, shorten-
sugar   ing, egg, baking soda, salt
½ cup vegetable   and vanilla. Process to mix,
shortening, divided   about 20 to 30 seconds.
in 4 pieces
1 egg
½ teaspoon baking
soda
½ teaspoon salt
½ teaspoon vanilla

1⅓ cups all-purpose . . . . .Add flour; Pulse just until
flour   mixed, 8 to 10 times.

(If flour is not completely mixed in, remove **Knife Blade**
and work in with hands.) Shape dough into 1-inch balls.
Place on ungreased cookie sheets. Flatten balls with
fork, crisscross fashion, to ¼-inch. Bake until golden
brown, about 10 to 12 minutes.

Makes 3½ dozen (2-inch) cookies

Peanut Chips and
Real Peanut-Butter Cookies

Spicy Oaties

SPICY OATIES ❧

¾ **cup packed** . . . . .Preheat oven to 350°F. Po-
brown sugar   sition **Knife Blade** in **Bowl.**
½ **cup vegetable**   Add sugar, shortening,
shortening   egg, milk, salt, baking
1 **egg**   soda, cinnamon and cloves.
2 **tablespoons milk**   Process to mix, about 15
½ **teaspoon salt**   seconds.
¼ **teaspoon baking**
soda
¼ **teaspoon cinnamon**
¼ **teaspoon ground**
cloves

1 **cup all-purpose flour** . . .Add remaining ingredients.
¾ **cup quick oats,**   Pulse just until mixed, about
uncooked   5 to 6 Pulses.
½ **cup raisins**
½ **cup walnuts**

Drop by slightly-rounded teaspoonfuls onto greased
cookie sheets. Bake for 12 to 14 minutes.

Makes 3½ dozen (1½-inch) cookies

NUTTY HALF MOONS ❧

1 **can (4½-oz.) whole,** . . . . .Position **Knife Blade** in
blanched almonds   **Bowl;** add almonds and
process until finely ground,
about 15 seconds. Trans-
fer to large mixing bowl.

2 **cups all-purpose** . . . . . .Add 1 cup flour and butter
flour, divided   to **Bowl;** process until but-
1 **cup butter, chilled,**   ter is cut into flour, about
cut in 1-inch pieces   15 seconds.

1 **cup sugar** . . . . .Add remaining 1 cup flour
and sugar; process to mix,
about 10 seconds.

1 **egg, slightly beaten** . . . . .Pour slightly beaten egg
evenly over butter mixture.

Process until dough is mixed, about 15 seconds. (If
dough is too dry, add 1 tablespoon water and process a
few seconds longer.) Add dough to ground almonds;
mix together with hands. Preheat oven to 350°F. Using a
¾-inch ball of dough for each cookie, shape into crescents.
Place on ungreased cookie sheets. Bake for 15 to 20
minutes. While warm, sprinkle with confectioners' sugar,
if desired.

Makes 7 dozen (1-inch) cookies

CHEWY MOLASSES COOKIES ❧

½ **cup molasses** . . . . .Preheat oven to 350°F. Po-
½ **cup vegetable oil**   sition **Knife Blade** in **Bowl.**
½ **cup sugar**   Add molasses, oil, sugar,
1 **egg**   egg, cinnamon, baking
1 **teaspoon cinnamon**   soda, ginger and salt to
½ **teaspoon baking**   **Bowl.** Process to mix, about
soda   15 seconds.
½ **teaspoon ginger**
½ **teaspoon salt**

2 **cups all-purpose** . . . . . . .Add flour. Pulse just until
flour   flour is mixed in, about 4 to
5 Pulses.

Drop by heaping teaspoonfuls onto greased cookie
sheets. Bake 10 to 11 minutes.

Makes 2½ dozen (2-inch) cookies

Fruit Desserts

SHIMMERING FRESH FRUIT

½ cup sugar	In 12-inch or electric skillet combine sugar, cornstarch and mace. Stir to mix. Gradually add water; stir until smooth. Cook over low heat, stirring constantly, until sugar mixture thickens and becomes shiny. Remove skillet from heat.
2 tablespoons cornstarch	
¼ teaspoon mace	
1 cup cold water	
1 medium seedless orange, halved (page 36)	Position **Disc** in **Bowl** with **slicing side up.** Slice orange. Add orange to skillet and stir. Cook over low heat for 1 to 2 minutes. Remove from heat and allow to cool slightly.
1 pint fresh strawberries, hulled (page 43)	Position **Disc** in **Bowl** with **slicing side up.** Slice strawberries and bananas. Add sliced fruit and grapes to skillet. Gently stir to coat fruit, being careful not to break fruit. Carefully spoon fruit mixture into 6 compote dishes. Garnish tops with fresh whole strawberries, if desired.
2 bananas, peeled, cut in half crosswise (page 20)	
½ pound seedless green grapes, removed from stem	

Makes 6 (1-cup) servings

FRESH APPLESAUCE

1 tablespoon lemon juice	Position **Knife Blade** in **Bowl.** Add juice, water, sugar and candies.
1 tablespoon water	
1 to 2 tablespoons sugar	
1 to 3 teaspoons red cinnamon candies	
2 medium apples, quartered, cored (peeled, if desired)	Position **Disc** in **Bowl** over **Knife Blade,** with **slicing side up;** slice apples.

Process about 10 seconds; remove **Disc.** Stir down sides of **Bowl.** Continue processing until apples are finely chopped, about 20 to 25 seconds.

Makes 1¼ cups

Shimmering Fresh Fruit

Smooth 'N Luscious Cheesecake

SMOOTH 'N LUSCIOUS CHEESECAKE

18 2½-inch graham cracker squares ¼ cup sugar ¼ cup butter or margarine, melted	Position **Knife Blade** in **Bowl** with **Disc** above it, **shredding side up.** Crumb crackers (page 21). Add sugar and butter to crumbs. Process until mixed, 4 to 5 seconds. Press mixture firmly into bottom and 2 inches up sides of 8-inch springform pan. Chill.
12 ounces soft cream cheese, cut in 1-inch pieces 3 egg yolks	Preheat oven to 350°F. Position **Knife Blade** in **Bowl.** Add cream cheese and egg yolks; process until smooth, about 10 seconds.
½ cup cream ½ cup sugar 2 tablespoons all-purpose flour 1 teaspoon lemon juice ½ teaspoon vanilla	Add cream, sugar, flour, lemon juice and vanilla. Process until well mixed, about 10 seconds. Turn off; scrape down **Bowl;** Pulse 2 to 3 seconds more. Remove **Knife Blade.**
3 egg whites	With mixer, whip egg whites until stiff, but not dry.

Fold egg whites into cream cheese mixture in **Bowl.** Pour into crust. Bake until cake springs back when touched lightly in center, 50 to 60 minutes. Chill well. Garnish with your favorite fruit topping, if desired.

Makes 1 (8-inch) cheesecake
(about 8 to 10 servings)

STRAWBERRY SHORTCAKE

1 pint fresh strawberries*, hulled	Position **Disc** in **Bowl** with **slicing side up;** slice strawberries.
2 tablespoons sugar	Sprinkle with sugar; let stand 1 hour.
4 Shortcake Biscuits (page 147)	Split Shortcake Biscuits and warm, if desired. Place two biscuit halves on each of 4 dessert plates.
1 cup whipping cream 1 to 2 tablespoons confectioners' sugar	Cover each biscuit with about ⅓ cup strawberries. Position **Knife Blade** in **Bowl.** Add cream and sugar. Process until thickened (page 26). Top with whipped cream.

Makes 4 shortcakes

*Sliced fresh peaches or a combination of bananas and strawberries may be substituted for berries.

NOTE: Any leftover biscuits may be frozen for future use.

APPLE CRISP

6 medium cooking apples, peeled, cored, quartered	Preheat oven to 375°F. Position **Disc** in **Bowl** with **slicing side up;** slice apples. As slices reach Fill Level, empty **Bowl** into ungreased 9-inch square baking pan.
2 tablespoons lemon juice	Sprinkle lemon juice over apples.
1 cup quick oats, uncooked ¾ cup packed brown sugar ½ cup all-purpose flour ½ cup butter or margarine, chilled, cut in 6 pieces 1 teaspoon cinnamon	Position **Knife Blade** in **Bowl;** add remaining ingredients. Process until crumbly, about 10 seconds. Crumble evenly over apples. Bake until apples are tender, 40 to 45 minutes. Serve warm or cold, plain or with ice cream or sweetened whipped cream.

Makes 6 (¾-cup) servings

NOTE: Substitute 5 to 6 cups fruits in season such as peaches or rhubarb. With rhubarb, add ½ cup sugar to fruit.

SHORTCAKE BISCUITS 〜

2 cups all-purpose flour	Preheat oven to 450°F. Position **Knife Blade** in **Bowl**;
1 tablespoon baking powder	add flour, baking powder, sugar, salt and butter. Pro-
1 tablespoon sugar	cess until particles are fine,
½ teaspoon salt	about 15 seconds.
¼ cup butter or margarine, chilled, cut in 3 pieces	
1 egg	Add egg to milk; beat slight-
½ cup milk	ly with fork.

With Processor running, add egg mixture, all at once, through food chute. Process until dough begins to form a ball, about 7 seconds. Dough will be slightly sticky. Knead 10 times on floured surface. Pat or roll out to ½-inch thickness. Cut into rounds with 2½-inch floured cutter or glass. Place on ungreased cookie sheet and bake until golden brown, about 10 to 12 minutes.

Makes 12 biscuits

STRAWBERRY FILLED DESSERT CREPES 〜

1 recipe Basic Blender Crepes (page 129)	Prepare crepes according to recipe.
1 quart (4 cups) fresh strawberries, hulled	Position **Disc** in **Bowl** with **slicing side up;** slice strawberries.
¼ cup confectioners' sugar	Sprinkle berries with confectioners' sugar and stir. Place about ¼ cup berries on each crepe. Roll up.
Sweetened whipped cream	Serve immediately plain or topped with sweetened whipped cream.

Makes 6 servings
(allowing 2 crepes per serving)

NOTE: Crepes and strawberries may be prepared in advance. Do not fill crepes more than an hour before serving.

VARIATION:
Fruit Filled Crepes: Substitute raspberries, blueberries, sliced peaches, sliced bananas or a combination for the strawberries.

QUICK FUDGE SAUCE 🥛

1 package (6-oz.) semi-sweet chocolate chips	Place chocolate chips in **Blender Jar.**
¼ cup light cream	In 1-quart saucepan, com-
¼ cup water	bine cream, water and
2 tablespoons sugar	sugar; bring to a boil.

Add to chips. Cover; blend at Blend speed until smooth, about 1 minute. Makes a thick and creamy sauce.

Makes 1 cup sauce

CITY GIRL FRUIT TRIFLE 🥄〜

A variation of an old English dessert which is sure to get requests for second helpings!

1 quart strawberries,* hulled	Position **Disc** in **Bowl** with **slicing side up.** Slice strawberries; transfer to
2 tablespoons confectioners' sugar	large mixing bowl; combine with sugar.
1 cup milk	Rinse **Bowl**. Position **Knife**
1 cup sour cream	**Blade** in **Bowl**. Add milk,
1 package (3¾-oz.) vanilla instant pudding	sour cream and pudding. Process 5 seconds; scrape down sides of **Bowl** and process 5 seconds more. Do not overprocess. Mixture will thicken in about 1 minute.
1 package (10¾-oz.) poundcake, frozen	Slice poundcake by hand into ¼-inch slices; position half the slices into the bottom and partially up sides of a 3-quart casserole or serving dish. Slices may overlap slightly.
4 tablespoons sherry or orange juice	Drizzle with 2 tablespoons sherry. Cover with half of the pudding and then half the strawberries. Repeat layers using remaining cake slices, sherry, pudding and fruit.
1 cup heavy cream	In small mixing bowl, com-
2 tablespoons confectioners' sugar	bine heavy cream and confectioners' sugar.

Using mixer, whip cream until stiff. Decorate surface of Trifle with large dollops of whipped cream or flute through pastry tube. Refrigerate until ready to serve.

Makes 12 (¾-cup) servings

*Peaches, blueberries, or various combinations may be used. Do not slice blueberries.

BLUEBERRY SYRUP 〜

1 cup fresh or frozen and thawed blueberries	Position **Knife Blade** in **Bowl**; add blueberries, water, sugar and corn-
1 cup water	starch. Process until well
¾ cup sugar	mixed, about 1 minute. Pour
1 tablespoon cornstarch	mixture into a 1½-quart saucepan; simmer until slightly thickened, about 2 minutes.
2 tablespoons lemon juice	Stir in lemon juice. Cool and refrigerate.

Makes about 1½ cups

CRANBERRY DESSERT FLUFF 🌀🐟

This refreshing dessert can be made well in advance. For a special touch, serve in compote dishes.

2 cups (½-lb.) fresh or frozen and thawed cranberries
2 cups miniature marshmallows
1 can (8-oz.) crushed pineapple, undrained
½ cup sugar . . . . .Position **Disc** in **Bowl** with **shredding side up;** shred cranberries. Transfer to large mixing bowl. Add marshmallows, pineapple and sugar.

½ cup walnuts . . . . .Position **Knife Blade** in **Bowl.** Add walnuts. Pulse to chop coarsely. Add to cranberries.

½ cup heavy cream . . . . .Position **Knife Blade** in **Bowl** (it doesn't have to be cleaned). Add heavy cream; process until thickened (page 26). Fold into cranberry mixture. Cover; refrigerate several hours or overnight.

Makes 8 (½-cup) servings

Orange Ice

BAKED PLUM PUDDING 🐟

A simple modern version of this traditional Christmas treat

4 slices fresh sandwich bread, quartered (page 14) . . . . .Preheat oven to 375°F. Position **Knife Blade** in **Bowl.** Add bread. Process until finely crumbed, about 15 seconds. Transfer to large mixing bowl.

1 cup pecans . . . . .Position **Knife Blade** in
2 cups raisins **Bowl.** Add pecans. Pulse
½ cup all-purpose flour to chop. Add pecans, raisins and flour to bread crumbs. Stir to mix.

1 cup sugar . . . . .Position **Knife Blade** in
½ cup butter, chilled, cut in 6 pieces **Bowl.** Add sugar, butter,
5 eggs eggs and seasonings. Pro-
2½ teaspoons cinnamon cess to mix thoroughly,
½ teaspoon allspice about 20 seconds. Stir into
¼ teaspoon ground cloves bread crumb mixture. Pour into greased, 2-quart casserole.

Bake for 30 minutes. Serve hot with Processor Hard Sauce.

Makes 10 (½-cup) servings

PROCESSOR HARD SAUCE 🐟

¼ cup soft butter, divided in 4 pieces . . . . . . .Position **Knife Blade** in
1 cup confectioners' sugar **Bowl.** Add all ingredients.
2 tablespoons brandy Process until smooth, 30
½ teaspoon cinnamon seconds. Turn off; scrape down sides of **Bowl.** Process 15 seconds longer.

Makes ¾ cup

ORANGE ICE 🥤

1 can (6-oz.) frozen orange juice concentrate . . . . .Add orange juice, water
½ orange juice can water and sugar to **Blender Jar.**
3 to 4 tablespoons confectioners' sugar Cover and blend at Crush Ice speed for 5 seconds.

7 to 10 standard-size ice cubes (15 to 20 small 1×1-inch cubes) (page 153) . . .With Blender running at Crush Ice speed, add ice cubes through lid insert, 2 to 3 at a time.

Blend until thick and smooth, 1 to 2 minutes. Turn off and stir down mixture frequently, 7 to 8 times. (This helps blend the ice evenly.) Serve immediately.

Makes 4 (½-cup) servings

Candies

SHORT CUT ROCKY ROAD CANDY

1 cup butterscotch flavored chips **1 cup semi-sweet chocolate chips** **1 can (14-oz.) sweetened condensed milk**	In 2-quart saucepan combine butterscotch and chocolate chips with condensed milk. Heat over medium low heat, stirring until chips are melted. (Be careful; do not let chocolate burn.) Remove from heat.
2 cups walnuts	Position **Disc** in **Bowl** with **slicing side up;** slice walnuts.
2 cups miniature marshmallows	Stir nuts and marshmallows into chocolate mixture.

Spread into greased 9-inch square baking pan. Refrigerate until firm, about 2 hours. Cut into squares.

Makes 2 pounds candy

NO BAKE CANDY LOAF

7 ounces (about 4 cups) whole vanilla wafers or 34 graham cracker squares, broken in half	Grease a 9×5-inch loaf pan. Line with aluminum foil and grease again. Set aside. Position **Knife Blade** in **Bowl** with **Disc** above it, **shredding side up.** Process to crumb finely (page 21). (Should make about 2½ cups crumbs.) Transfer to large mixing bowl.
1 cup walnuts or other nuts **1 cup raisins or chopped dates** **2 cups (1 lb.) mixed chopped candied fruit**	Position **Disc** in **Bowl** with **slicing side up.** Slice nuts. Add nuts and fruit to crumbs. Mix well.
3 cups miniature marshmallows **1 small can (⅔ cup) evaporated milk** **1 tablespoon rum or brandy** **1 teaspoon vanilla**	Position **Knife Blade** in **Bowl.** Add marshmallows, milk and flavorings. Process until mixture is smooth, about 2 minutes.

Pour over fruit. Stir until evenly combined. Press firmly into prepared loaf pan. Decorate top with nuts, candied fruit or maraschino cherries. Cover and refrigerate 2 days before serving.

Makes 1 (9×5-inch) loaf

Short Cut Rocky Road Candy

Bittersweet Candied Orange Peel

BITTERSWEET CANDIED ORANGE PEEL ◖

2 large, thick-skinned . . . . Cut peel on each orange
oranges into quarter sections; care-
fully remove from orange
without breaking sections.
Reserve oranges for other
use. Pack into bottom of
food chute, cut side down.
Position **Disc** in **Bowl** with
slicing side up; using light
pressure, slice peel. Cut
peel remaining on top of
Disc into strips by hand.
Repeat with remaining
peel. Place peel in 2-quart
saucepan; cover with cold
water. Simmer until tender,
about 10 minutes. Drain;
set aside.

¾ cup sugar . . . . Combine sugar, water and
¼ cup water corn syrup in same 2-quart
1 tablespoon light saucepan. Stir over low
corn syrup heat until sugar is dissolved. Add peel; simmer
until syrup is thick, 20 to 25
minutes. Drain in strainer
and spread peel on wax
paper to dry, about 1 to 1½
hours.

2 to 3 tablespoons . . . . Roll in or sprinkle with sug-
sugar ar to coat.

Makes about 2 cups

HOW TO MAKE CANDIED ORANGE PEEL ◖

Cut peel on oranges in quarters;
gently peel. Pack in chute, cut side
down, curving slightly to fit chute.

Position Disc in Bowl, slicing side up.
Slice peel with light pressure. Simmer
until tender and drain.

Dissolve sugar in water and corn
syrup. Add peel and simmer until
syrup is thick (see recipe).

Strawberry Milk Shake

Thirst-Quenching
Beverages

Prepare punch for a party, a shake for a snack, even a one-glass meal. Here's another place where the Food Processor and Blender help you any time of the day.

RICH 'N CREAMY MILK SHAKE

⅓ cup milk . . . .
2 large scoops ice
   cream (about 1 cup)
1 teaspoon malted milk
   powder (optional)
	Place all ingredients in **Blender Jar.** Cover; blend at Purée speed until smooth, thick and frothy, 1 to 2 minutes. (Check after 45 seconds.)

Makes 1 large shake
(about 1 cup)

VARIATIONS:
Banana Nut: Add 1 medium, ripe banana, cut in 1-inch pieces, and 8 to 10 walnut halves. Blend as above. Makes 1½ cups.

Coffee: Add 2 tablespoons brown sugar, 1 teaspoon instant coffee, and a pinch of nutmeg. Blend as above. Makes 1½ cups.

Date Nut: Combine 6 soft pitted dates, halved, and ¼ cup hot water or coffee. Blend to a purée. Add milk, ice cream, 1 tablespoon brown sugar or honey and 6 nut halves (walnuts, pecans, filberts). Blend as above. Makes 1½ cups.

Strawberry: Add ½ cup fresh strawberries and a pinch of nutmeg or mace. Blend as above. Makes 1½ cups.

BREAKFAST EGGNOG

1 cup milk . . . . 1 egg 1 teaspoon vanilla Nutmeg	Add milk, egg and vanilla to **Blender Jar.** Cover and blend at Liquefy speed for 45 to 50 seconds. Pour into large glass. Sprinkle top with nutmeg.

Makes 1 (1½-cup) serving

FROSTY LEMON FRAPPÉ

1 can (6-oz.) frozen lemonade concentrate, pink or white, partially defrosted	Place all ingredients in **Blender Jar.** Blend at Crush Ice speed for 30 seconds. Pour into decorative glasses, serve immediately.
2 juice cans ice water	
10 large ice cubes	

Makes 3½ cups

BLUSHING FRUIT PUNCH

A sweet, festive punch.

1 package (10-oz.) frozen strawberries, partially thawed	In **Blender Jar,** combine strawberries, pineapple and lemonade. Blend at Blend speed until smooth, about 1 minute. Chill until ready to serve.
1 can (13-oz.) crushed pineapple, undrained	
1 can (6-oz.) frozen lemonade concentrate, partially thawed	
2 bottles (16-oz. each) ginger ale, chilled	Just before serving, stir in ginger ale. Serve over ice cubes.

Makes about 2 quarts

Frosty Lemon Frappé made with pink lemonade concentrate

HOW TO CHOP ICE IN BEVERAGES

Add ice cubes (1 to 6) to liquid in Blender Jar. Do not exceed 36-ounce mark on Jar. Cover.

Blend at Crush Ice speed until ice is chopped to desired texture.

Serve and repeat for additional drinks.

152

FLAVORED ICE CONES 🥤

8 to 10 standard-size ..... With Blender running at
ice cubes (16 to 20 Crush Ice speed, drop ice
small 1×1-inch cubes through lid insert,
cubes-see below) one at a time, into **Blender**
4 paper cups or cones **Jar.** Crush no more than
(6-oz. size) 5 cubes at a time. Mound
crushed ice into 6-ounce
paper cups or cones. Re-
peat with remaining ice
cubes.

For flavoring, use ¼ cup flavored syrup (maple, rasp-
berry), or jelly, melted and cooled. Drizzle 2 tablespoons
syrup over each ice cone. See picture below.

Makes 4 cones

VARIATION:
Freeze your favorite fruit drink in ice cube trays and
crush following directions for Flavored Ice Cones.

TROPICAL FRUIT COOLER 🥤

1½ cups pineapple ...... Add all ingredients to
juice, unsweetened **Blender Jar.** Cover; blend
1 medium banana, at Crush Ice speed until ice
cut in 4 pieces is crushed and mixture is
4 standard-size ice smooth, about 15 seconds.
cubes (8 small Pour into decorative glass-
1×1-inch cubes) es. Serve immediately.

Makes 4 (6-ounce) servings

SPICY CUCUMBER COCKTAIL 🥤

1 small cucumber, ... Slice 4 ¼-inch slices from
unpeeled end of cucumber. Set aside
for garnish. Peel remaining
cucumber; cut in half
lengthwise; remove seeds
(page 27). Cut pieces in
half crosswise. Add to
Blender Jar.

2½ cups tomato juice .... Add remaining ingredients,
1 teaspoon lemon except ice cubes. Cover;
juice process at Crush Ice speed
1 teaspoon for 30 seconds. With Pro-
Worcestershire cessor still running, add
sauce ice cubes through lid insert,
½ to 1 teaspoon salt one at a time. Continue
⅛ teaspoon pepper blending until ice is crushed,
4 standard-size ice about 10 seconds. Pour in-
cubes (8 small to large decorative glasses.
1×1-inch cubes) Garnish edge of glasses
with cucumber slices. Serve
immediately.

Makes 4 (8-ounce) servings

TO LIQUEFY FOODS

Add up to 2 cups of 1-inch cubed food, such as
carrots, and 2 cups liquid, such as water, to Blender
Jar. Cover and blend at Liquefy speed until smooth,
about 1 to 2 minutes. Always be sure to have equal
or higher amounts liquid to solids. The Blender can-
not extract juice from foods, but it can liquefy them
in water, milk, juices or broth.

HOW TO CRUSH ICE 🥤

Start Blender at Crush Ice speed; remove insert and drop up to 5 ice
cubes (1 at a time) through lid. Quickly replace insert.

Remove ice when crushed. Repeat if
more than 5 cubes of ice are needed.

For Flavored Ice Cones, pack ice into cups; drizzle with favorite syrup.

Frozen Daiquiri

FROZEN DAIQUIRI ▽

2 standard-size ice cubes (4 small 1×1-inch cubes)	. . . . .With Blender running at Crush Ice speed, remove lid insert and add ice cubes, one at a time. Replace insert and crush ice, about 5 seconds. Stir down ice from sides of **Jar.**
1½ ounces light rum 1 tablespoon lime juice 1 tablespoon sugar Dash maraschino cordial (optional)	. . . . .Add rum, lime juice, sugar and maraschino cordial to ice in **Blender Jar.** Cover.
3 to 4 standard-size ice cubes (5 to 6 small 1×1-inch cubes)	. . . . .With Blender running at Crush Ice speed, add ice cubes through lid insert. Replace insert and blend for 1 minute or more, until thick and smooth.

Stop and stir down mixture frequently, about 6 to 7 times; this helps to blend the ice evenly. Spoon into chilled glass. Top with maraschino cherry, if desired.

Makes 1 (8-ounce) frozen daiquiri

WHISKEY SOUR ▽

1½ ounces whiskey 1½ tablespoons lemon juice 1 to 2 teaspoons very fine sugar	. . . . .Add whiskey, lemon juice and sugar to **Blender Jar.** Cover.
1 standard-size ice cube (2 small 1×1-inch cubes)	. . . .With Blender running at Crush Ice speed, add ice cubes through lid insert. Replace insert and blend about 10 seconds longer. Pour into serving glass.
½ orange slice Maraschino cherry	. . . . .Garnish drink.

Makes 1 (4-ounce) drink

MARGARITA ▽

1 slice lime Coarse or regular salt	. . . . .Rub inside rim of chilled cocktail glass with lime. Pour salt into a saucer; dip moistened rim of glass into salt to lightly coat rim.
1½ ounces tequila ½ ounce cointreau or triple sec 2 tablespoons lime juice	. . . . .Add tequila, cointreau and lime juice to **Blender Jar.** Cover.
2 standard-size ice cubes (3 small 1×1-inch cubes)	. . . . .With Blender running at Crush Ice speed, add ice cubes through lid insert. Replace insert and blend 15 to 20 seconds longer. Pour into prepared serving glass.

Makes 1 (5-ounce) drink

EGGNOG ▽

2 standard-size ice cubes (3 small 1×1-inch cubes)	. . . . .With Blender running at Crush Ice speed, remove lid insert and add ice cubes. Replace insert and crush ice, about 5 seconds. Stir down ice from sides of **Jar.**
1½ ounces brandy or whiskey 2 to 3 teaspoons very fine sugar 1 egg 3 ounces heavy cream	. . . .Add brandy, sugar, egg and cream to ice in **Blender Jar.** Cover. Blend at Stir speed for about 10 seconds. Pour into serving glasses.
Nutmeg	. . . . .Sprinkle nutmeg on top of drinks.

Makes 2 (5-ounce) drinks

PINA COLADA

2 standard-size ice cubes (4 small 1×1-inch cubes)	With Blender running at Crush Ice speed, remove lid insert and add ice cubes. Replace insert and crush, about 5 seconds. Empty into 2 serving glasses.
2 standard-size ice cubes (4 small 1×1-inch cubes) **6 ounces unsweetened pineapple juice** **2 ounces light rum** **1 ounce cream of coconut** **1½ ounces heavy cream**	Repeat procedure above; leave ice in **Blender Jar** and stir down from sides. Add pineapple juice, rum, cream of coconut and cream to ice in **Blender Jar.** Cover. Blend at Stir speed, about 10 seconds. Pour into prepared serving glasses.
Maraschino cherries	Garnish drinks.

Makes 2 (5-ounce) drinks served over crushed ice

GRASSHOPPER

2 standard-size ice cubes (4 small 1×1-inch cubes)	With Blender running at Crush Ice speed, remove lid insert and add ice cubes. Replace insert and crush ice, about 5 seconds. Stir down ice from sides of **Jar.**
1½ ounces green creme de menthe **1 ounce white creme de cacao** **1½ ounces heavy cream**	Add creme de menthe, creme de cacao and cream to ice in **Blender Jar.** Cover. Blend at Stir speed about 10 seconds. Pour into serving glasses.

Makes 2 (3-ounce) drinks

BRANDY ALEXANDER

2 standard-size ice cubes (4 small 1×1-inch cubes)	With Blender running at Crush Ice speed, remove lid insert and add ice cubes. Replace insert and crush ice, about 5 seconds. Stir down ice from sides of **Jar.**
1½ ounces brandy **1 ounce white creme de cacao** **1½ ounces heavy cream**	Add brandy, creme de cacao and cream to ice in **Blender Jar.** Cover. Blend at Stir speed for about 10 seconds. Pour into serving glasses.

Makes 2 (3-ounce) drinks

HOT SPICY ORANGE TEA MIX

¾ cup powdered orange breakfast drink **1 cup unflavored instant tea*** **2 teaspoons cinnamon** **1 teaspoon nutmeg** **½ teaspoon allspice** **½ teaspoon ground cloves**	Add all ingredients to **Blender Jar.** Cover and blend at Crush Ice speed until smooth, 30 seconds. Wait a few seconds before removing lid for mix to settle. Store in tightly covered container.

To serve, add about 1 rounded teaspoon mix to coffee cup and fill with boiling water. Adjust amount to suit individual taste.

Makes about 1 cup (about 38 servings)

*Adjust amount, depending upon strength of flavor desired.

VIENNESE COFFEE

Keep handy when you want something different or extra special.

1 cup instant coffee **1 cup non-dairy powdered creamer** **2 teaspoons cinnamon** **⅛ teaspoon salt**	Place all ingredients in **Blender Jar.** Cover and blend at Crush Ice speed until smooth, 30 seconds.

Store in tightly covered container. To serve, add 2 teaspoons mix to a coffee cup and fill with boiling water. Adjust amount to suit individual taste. Top with dollops of sweetened whipped cream, if desired.

Makes about 1⅓ cups (about 32 servings)

Viennese Coffee

Index